Sources of Christianity

Also by Bastiaan Baan

The Chymical Wedding of Christian Rosenkreutz:
A Commentary on a Christian Path of Initiation

Lord of the Elements:
Interweaving Christianity and Nature

Old and New Mysteries:
From Trials to Initiation

Ways into Christian Meditation

Sources of Christianity
Peter, Paul and John

BASTIAAN BAAN,
CHRISTINE GRUWEZ
and JOHN VAN SCHAIK

Translated from Dutch by Philip Mees

First published in Dutch under the title
Bronnen van het christendom. Petrus, Paulus en Johannes
by Christofoor Publishers, Zeist in 2007
First published in English by Floris Books in 2017

© 2007 Uitgeverij Christofoor, Zeist
This translation © Floris Books 2017

All rights reserved. No part of this book may be reproduced in any form without written permission of Floris Books, Edinburgh
www.florisbooks.co.uk

Unless otherwise indicated, the quotations from the New Testament were taken from *The New Testament,* a rendering by John Madsen, Floris Books 1994
Those from the Old Testament were taken from the Revised Standard Version (RSV)

British Library CIP Data available
ISBN 978-178250-429-0
Printed and bound by Gutenberg Press Limited, Malta

Contents

Introduction   7

PART I Pre-Christian Streams

1 The Messianic Expectation in the Old Testament   13
John van Schaik

2 Mysteries and Initiation in the Greek World   27
Christine Gruwez

3 Messianic Expectation and the Essenes   45
Bastiaan Baan

PART II The Three Great Apostles

4 Peter the Builder of Churches   59
John van Schaik

5 Paul, in Whom Christ Lives   77
Christine Gruwez

6 John: The Imitation of Christ   97
Bastiaan Baan

PART III Early Christian Movements

7 Esoteric Petrine Christianity   115
John van Schaik

8 Dionysius the Areopagite, the First Christian Mystic   127
Christine Gruwez

9 Origen: A Life in Service of Wisdom   143
Bastiaan Baan

Notes   157
Bibliography   160
Glossary and Index   163

Among the three apostles, Peter may be compared with Moses. He is the lawgiver, the principle of stability, the foundation. To Paul applies what the book of Jesus Sirach says about Elijah: 'He erupted like fire, and his word burned like a torch.' Paul is the Elijah of the New Testament, the principle of movement, development, of freedom in the church. John may be compared with John the Baptist. Like the latter, he is an apostle of the future; he points to the future.

Friedrich Wilhelm Joseph Schelling (1775–1854)
Philosophie der Offenbarung, *lecture 36*

Introduction

Originally, Christianity did not have dogmas; it was a 'unity in diversity.' The twelve apostles each understood and interpreted Jesus Christ in their own individual ways. This explains why Christianity developed a very different form in India (where it goes back to the apostle Thomas) from the way it grew, for instance, in Russia (where the foundation was laid by the apostle Andrew).

Besides the twelve views developed by the twelve apostles, history has always recognized three principal apostles who inaugurated the three fundamental and essential forms of Christianity: Peter, Paul and John. Thus, for instance, the philosopher and theologian Schelling distinguishes Petrine, Pauline and Johannine Christianity.[1]

This book is the result of a series of lectures in 2006/7 on these three forms of Christianity. John van Schaik gave the lectures on Petrine Christianity, Christine Gruwez on Pauline Christianity, and Bastiaan Baan on Johannine Christianity.

In three groups of three lectures each, we tried to trace the development of Christianity. First, we searched for pre-Christian sources that were available to these three apostles. Of course they connected, each in their own way, to streams that existed already before Christianity. In their manifestation, they show aspects of their own natures. Thus Peter builds on the foundation of Old Testament language and imagery so as to anchor Christianity in the Jewish tradition. Paul, who grew up as a Jew in Hellenistic culture, connects with Greek thought and becomes the 'apostle to the heathens'. And John, the author of the most spiritual gospel builds on streams that are oriented toward the future, such as that of the Essenes with their apocalyptic scriptures.

During the lectures, which we prepared and reviewed together, it became clear that we often approached a particular theme in very different ways. These differences did not diminish our collaboration, but strengthened it. Pursuing an independent and free path of thought and spirit, the three authors were able to put 'unity in diversity' into practice. This does not mean that each of us always fully subscribes to the contributions of the other two, but that we were able to view each other's approach with growing respect. By this method of freely commenting on each other's work, a palette of different styles and views has emerged.

In the first three chapters, three religious streams are described that each have their own character. In these, one can easily recognize the trichotomy of spirit, soul and body.

The second series of three chapters describes the activity of the three apostles in their own time and culture.

The final three chapters go into how the characteristics of Peter, Paul and John are manifested in forms of early esoteric Christianity. We do not consider the question which of the different churches reflect these characteristics; that would be a study in itself.

One might also ask in what ways these streams are still working today, but this is a theme that is dealt with more implicitly in all chapters, rather than receiving special emphasis.

The three approaches to Christianity are not only interesting from a psychological point of view, but it seems as if a supra-personal element wants to come to expression in the three different views. This element is also incorporated in the different contributions more implicitly than explicitly.

Finally, in the different Messianic expectations in the Old Testament we recognized a certain trinity that led the three apostles Peter, Paul and John to develop different views of the Messiah – not in the sense of mutually exclusive theologies, but in the sense of unity in diversity. This discovery was a great inspiration to us: that each of these three streams complements the other two, and even needs the other two to approach the reality of Jesus Christ.

There is one being that can truly say, 'I am the truth' (Jn 14:6). When people with their inevitable limitations, collaborate, more than the work of all the individuals is able to come to light. We view this book as an effort to arrive, through collaboration, at more than the sum of the parts. At any rate, we inspired each other to come to new ways of looking at things and ideas, which are documented in this book.

Bastiaan Baan

PART I
Pre-Christian Streams

1
The Messianic Expectation in the Old Testament
John van Schaik

And he began to teach them: 'The Son of Man must suffer much and be rejected by the elders and the chief priests and the scribes; and he will be killed and will rise again after three days.'

(Mark 8:31)

From myth to history – from Elohim to YHWH

The Old Testament is the story in which space becomes time. Surrounded by peoples who were living in a mythical space-consciousness of the spiritual world, the Jewish people committed to the earth and to time. The Old Testament is the story in which God works in the history of the Jewish people.[1] In the ancient mystery cultures the connection with the divine world was maintained by the initiates of the mystery temples, such as Ephesus in Greece (now Efes in Turkey), the Egyptian initiations, and the Babylonian mystery cults. From Babylon the cult of Baal was exported to the land of the Jews, as was the cult of the Queen of Heaven who was usually called Astarte by the surrounding peoples. But YHWH and the prophets wanted nothing to do with her and were merciless. The prophet Elijah had 450 priests of Baal executed (1 K 18), and YHWH complained about the Queen of Heaven. In Jeremiah 7:17f YHWH said:

> Do you not see what they are doing in the cities of Judah and in the streets of Jerusalem? The children gather wood, the fathers kindle fire, and the women knead dough, to make cakes for the

queen of heaven; and they pour out drink offerings to other gods, to provoke me to anger.

That was the seventh century before Christ; the century when the Jewish people made their decisive turn to monotheism.[2] This turn to monotheism began with Moses. In the burning bush, the God of Israel revealed his name for the first time:

I appeared to Abraham, to Isaac, and to Jacob, as God Almighty [*El Shaddai*] but by my name the LORD I did not make myself known to them (Ex 6:3).*

Initially, YHWH, as El Shaddai, was but one of the gods in the pantheon of the great god El. Psalm 82:1 says:

God has taken his place in the divine council; in the midst of the gods he holds judgment.

El, or Elyon, assigned a people to each of the gods of his pantheon. In Deuteronomy (32:8f) we read:

When the Most High gave to the nations their inheritance, when he separated the sons of men, he fixed the bounds of the peoples according to the number of the sons of God. For the LORD's portion is his people, Jacob his allotted heritage.

In this pantheon, YHWH even had a feminine partner with the name of Asherah. Quite a number of artifacts have been found in which 'YHWH with his Asherah' is invoked. Asherah was the same as Astarte, the Queen of Heaven. In the course of Jewish history, however, YHWH became a jealous god and no longer tolerated anyone beside himself:

For you shall worship no other god, for the LORD, whose name is Jealous, is a jealous God (Ex 34:14).

---

* In most English versions of the Old Testament the word LORD in capitals indicates the Hebrew YHWH.

As time went on, the Jews attributed characteristics to YHWH that used to be attributed only to El. They turned the Gods (Elohim – plural) into one God. That is the essence of the monotheism of the Jews.

The history of the Jewish people went from an eternal pantheon to the historical one God. There was no place for initiates and mysteries. Contact with YHWH was maintained by the prophets. God revealed himself to them because God called them, not because they were initiated. The Old Testament is the story of the relationship the people had with their God, with YHWH. The prophets guarded this relationship and told the people what its quality was.

Yahwism and Judaism

The last prophet of the people of Israel was Malachi who lived around 470 BC. After him there were no more prophets. With Malachi a particular tradition of Judaism came to an end, a tradition that may be called Yahwism. After Malachi began what is often called Judaism, which is characterized by contact with and influence by Hellenism, culminating in the conquest of Judea by Alexander the Great in 333 BC. Chaim Potok calls this moment in Jewish history 'a jolt to the West.'[3]

In the fourth century BC the Old Testament books, Chronicles, were written. In Chronicles, the prophets are no longer the leaders of the people; they have been replaced by the High Priests. The priests rewrote the old story; in biblical scholarship they are called the priestly editors, while the old Yahwist tradition was written by the Yahwist editors. Genesis 2 – Yahweh creates – would then have been written by a Yahwist, while Genesis 1 – the Elohim create – was written by the priestly tradition. For this reason, the priestly editors are sometimes also called an Elohists. The two biblical books of Chronicles, were written by a priest. This is proven in part by the fact that, compared with other Bible books, in Chronicles the name of God, YHWH, is more often replaced by Elohim.

The Messianic expectations of the Yahwist and the Elohist

The story of the Old Testament is not merely the story of the myth that became history, and of the movement from polytheism to monotheism, it is also the story of the Messianic expectation. The entire Old Testament is permeated by the hope of redemption and a better (final) future. And it goes without saying that the Yahwist and priestly traditions each had their own picture of the Messiah. We will see later that the Messianic expectation of the Yahwist was more of an earthly Messiah, most often a king. On the other hand, the Elohist longed for a priest-Messiah, or even YHWH who redeems. We will examine these two Messianic expectations in the Old Testament.

The Son of Man of Daniel

But to make things even more complicated, in the Book of Daniel there is mention of a third Messiah, the 'Son of Man.' The Book of Daniel tells of the prophet Daniel who is said to have lived during the Babylonian exile, but the book itself was written around 165 BC. Daniel had a vision:

> I saw in the night visions, and behold, with the clouds of heaven there came one like a son of man, and he came to the Ancient of Days and was presented before him. And to him was given dominion and glory and kingdom, that all peoples, nations, and languages should serve him; his dominion is an everlasting dominion, which shall not pass away, and his kingdom one that shall not be destroyed. (Dan 7:13f).

Daniel saw a heavenly figure, a Son of Man, who would establish his reign. This was something new in Judaism. The book of Daniel introduced a new type of Messiah, that of the Son of Man who seems to appear straight from heaven. It looks as if this Son of Man takes no notice of history at all. The Son of Man, as it were, bursts vertically into the horizontal line of the classical Jewish Messianic expectation.

The Book of Daniel is apocalyptic literature, a new genre that developed around 200 BC. Apocalyptic literature was popular with the Essenes, among others, and the Book of Revelation also belongs to this genre.

Thus we have the following picture:

- Until about 400 BC we witness Yahwism;
- From about 400 to 200 BC we witness the Judaism of the priests; and
- From about 200 BC apocalyptic literature is added to these two.

We have now traced no less than three Messiah representations: a king, a priest and a divine Son of Man. The Jews believed that the kingly and priestly Messiah would come from the Jewish people – a son of David – and would appear as a historical person. The Son of Man, however, would come directly out of heaven.[4]

The Messiah: king or priest?

The priestly Messiah appeared on the stage in the Old Testament when the people were being oppressed, while during times of prosperity the emphasis was on a king from the line of David. In the priestly expectation it was sometimes YHWH himself who saved the people. This appears in a number of places in the book of Isaiah:

> Hark, your watchmen lift up their voice, together they sing for joy; for eye to eye they see the return of the LORD to Zion. Break forth together in singing, you waste places of Jerusalem; for the LORD has comforted his people, he has redeemed Jerusalem. (Is 52:8f).

But most of the time God made use of a servant. Sometimes that was King David, who then, however, received priestly traits, such as in Jeremiah and Ezekiel at the time of the oppression in Babylonian exile:

PART I: PRE-CHRISTIAN STREAMS

> And I, the L ORD, will be their God, and my servant David shall be prince among them; I, the L ORD, have spoken. 'I will make with them a covenant of peace ...' (Ez 34:24f).

In times of prosperity, the emphasis was on David as sovereign ruler, the ideal king who united North and South Israel:

> Of the increase of his government and of peace there will be no end, upon the throne of David, and over his kingdom, to establish it, and to uphold it with justice and with righteousness from this time forth and for evermore. (Is 9:7).

Thus we see that in the Old Testament David is sometimes described as the servant of the Lord, and sometimes as a sovereign ruler.

Two Messiahs: a priest and a king

The Old Testament does not always speak of a priestly *or* a kingly Messiah. Sometimes the appearance of two anointed ones (the word Messiah means 'anointed') at the same time is mentioned. For instance, Zechariah said (4:11–14):

> Then I said to him, 'What are these two olive trees on the right and left of the lampstand?' And a second time I said to him, 'What are these two branches of the olive trees, which are beside the two golden pipes from which the gold is poured out?' He said to me, 'Do you not know what these are?' I said, 'No, my lord.' Then he said, 'These are the two anointed who stand by the Lord of the whole earth.'

Two anointed ones who worked together during the reconstruction of the temple after the Babylonian captivity. Zechariah spoke here of Zerubbabel, from the line of David, *and* of the priest Joshua. In 515 BC the temple was rededicated (Ezra 6:13–22). But Israel remained under the yoke of Persia. The Kingdom of Israel was not restored; Zerubbabel did not become King of the Jews. He mysteriously disappeared from the stage. Only Joshua, the priest, remained. The Messianic longing projected by Zechariah into the two anointed ones, Zerubbabel and Joshua, was not realised. But the idea of two Messiahs acting in concert remained alive.

It lived in the rabbis at the time of Christ. They were familiar with the image of two Messiahs appearing simultaneously. In the Talmud we can read about Messiah-ben-Joseph, who was connected with the ten tribes of North Israel *and* Messiah-ben-David, who was associated with Judah and the dynasty of David. First Messiah-ben-Joseph appears, who will suffer and die, but is then brought back to life by the Messiah-ben-David. The story of these two Messiahs is rather fragmentary in the Talmud, but in the tenth century AD all the fragments were put together into one story by Rabbi Gaon:

> At that time a man will arise from the Children of Joseph ... and he will be called Messiah of God. And many people will gather around him in Upper Galilee, and he will be their king. ... And when Messiah ben Joseph and all the people with him will dwell in Jerusalem, Armilus [the Anti-Christ] will hear their tiding and will come and make magic and sorcery to lead many astray with them, and he will go up and wage war against Jerusalem, and will defeat Messiah ben Joseph and his people, and will kill many of them. ... When Messiah ben Joseph is killed, his body will remain cast out [in the streets] for forty days, but no unclean thing will touch him, until Messiah ben David comes and brings him back to life, as commanded by the Lord. And this will be the beginning of the signs which he will perform, and this is the resurrection of the dead which will come to pass.[5]

We also come across the idea of two Messiahs in late esoteric Jewish writings such as the Hebrew Book of Enoch from the first to third century after Christ:

> And I saw Messiah, son of Joseph, and his generation and their works and their doings that they will do against the nations of the world. And I saw Messiah, son of David, and his generation, and all the fights and wars, and all the fights and wars, and their

works and their doings that they will do with Israel both for good and evil.⁶

And in the Zohar, a mystical Jewish document from the Middle Ages, we find the following:

> The son of David and the son of Joseph are two, not one. The son of Joseph will die a cruel death. Then the son of David shall follow him. The Messiah, who is the son of Joseph, will be united with the son of David, but he will be slain.
>
> Another Messiah, the son of Joseph, shall unite with the Messiah, the son of David. But the Messiah, the son of Joseph, will not remain alive; he will be slain and will come alive again when the little mound receives light on the great mound.
>
> The Messiah, son of David, and the Messiah, son of Joseph, have fallen into the abyss. One of them is a poor man riding on a donkey; the other is the firstborn of a bull.⁷

The words 'the first-born of a bull' indicate a king or ruler. We can conclude that the image of the two Messiahs was consistently present throughout Jewish history, at any rate into the Middle Ages. Rabbis spoke of it in the Talmud and Jewish mystics in the Zohar.

The Messiah: priest-king

The image of the Messiah who is king *or* priest in some cases refers to David. He is then priest (servant) *or* king, as we have seen. But there are also passages in the Old Testament in which king and priest have become one in David. He is then not priest *or* king, but priest *and* king. The sovereign king David is then at the same time a humble king, according to Zechariah. For that reason, Zechariah has him come on an donkey (Zech 9:9). By order of God, he receives a priestly anointment from Samuel (1 Sam 16), but he is also anointed as king of Israel by the elders of the people:

Then all the tribes of Israel came to David at Hebron, and said, 'Behold, we are your bone and flesh. In times past, when Saul was king over us, it was you that led out and brought in Israel; and the Lord said to you, "You shall be shepherd of my people Israel, and you shall be prince over Israel".' So all the elders of Israel came to the king at Hebron; and King David made a covenant with them at Hebron before the Lord, and they anointed David king over Israel. (2 Sam 5:1–3).

Since that time, the image of the priest-king always remained an ideal in old Israel. The enigmatic King Melchizedek of Salem was a kind of archetypal image for this, since he was both king and priest of the Most High:

And Melchizedek king of Salem brought out bread and wine; he was priest of God Most High (Gen 14:18).

And yet, after David, the ideal of the priest-king was not again realised in the history of Israel. Only in the second century BC was there another priest-king: among the Hasmonean (Maccabean) kings. The Hasmonean rulers let themselves be ordained as priests, even as high priests. According to tradition, however, this was illegitimate, for the Hasmonean rulers did not belong to the priestly line of Zadok, the priest of David and Solomon. These priest-kings reigned from about 150 BC to the desecration of the temple by the Romans in 63 BC. They had great military successes, witness John-Hyrcanus I, who reigned but one year and reunited the North and South Kingdoms of Israel. Because of that he called himself king, but this was improper since the Hasmoneans were not sons of David. So they were severely criticised by orthodox Jews. As a result, these orthodox Jews were persecuted by the Hasmonean rulers, and many fled into the desert, including the Essenes. The Hasmoneans were also in favour of Hellenisation, and for the Essenes they had therefore become instruments of Satan. The Essenes no longer came to the temple in Jerusalem.

Jesus – two Messiahs plus a third

Let us summarise. Around the year one there clearly were two Messianic expectations in classical Judaism: the kingly Messiah from the house of David and the priestly Messiah from the house of Joseph. The Messiah-ben-Joseph was to be a suffering servant, as prophesied in Isaiah:

> He had no form or comeliness that we should look at him, and no beauty that we should desire him.
> He was despised and rejected by men; a man of sorrows, and acquainted with grief;
> ... he was wounded for our transgressions, he was bruised for our iniquities ... He was oppressed and he was afflicted. (Is 53:2–7)

He would be a priest-prophet. The Elohist often proposed that this would be Elijah come again, for Elijah did not die, he was taken up by God.

And thus some of Jesus' apostles thought that he was Elijah returned (Mk 8:27f). But the people viewed Jesus as the king. During the entry into Jerusalem the people sang, 'Blessed is he who comes, the King, in the name of the Lord' (Lk 19:38). They shouted, 'Hosanna, sing to the Son of David!' (Mt 21:9).

Up to this point, traditional Jews could follow it: Jesus as son of David and Jesus as the suffering servant/prophet. That was fine so far. But now something extraordinary happened: when Jesus started predicting his own suffering he did not do so as servant/prophet, but as Son of Man. That was unheard of:

> And he began to teach them: 'the Son of Man must suffer much and be rejected by the elders and the chief priests and the scribes; and he will be killed and will rise again after three days.' (Mk 8:31).

The Son of Man is a concept from Jewish esoteric imagery, from apocalyptic imagery. However, nothing is said of suffering and death. Jesus joined the Jewish picture of the two Messiahs to a third: that of the pre-existing Son of God. If Jesus had said, 'I am the prophet who has to suffer,' the Jews would have understood it. But it was impossible to understand that the Son of Man would have to suffer! It was the reason why Peter became so angry when Jesus, the Son of Man, predicted his own suffering. Jesus then said, 'Leave me, power of Satan' (Mt 16:23). And similarly, Judas Iscariot (the Zealot) became angry because he believed in the Davidian warrior-king who would liberate Israel by force: how can a warrior-king predict his own death!

The genealogies of Matthew and Luke

We thus have two Messiahs in the Old Testament, the Messiah-ben-David and the Messiah-ben-Joseph. And in the New Testament we find two extensive and very different genealogies of Jesus in Matthew and Luke. In Matthew, Jesus is represented as the son of a king. It is the story with the three kings. Luke, however, says that Jesus was born in a stable, and does not speak of kings but of shepherds. It is therefore fairly obvious to look for a relationship between Luke and the Messiah-ben-Joseph, and between Matthew and the Messiah-ben-David. Matthew described the kingly expectation of the Messiah, while Luke described the priestly Messiah. For after King David, Luke continued with Nathan the priest, but Matthew with David's other son, Solomon.[8]

Rudolf Steiner concluded from the two different genealogies that there indeed must have been two 'Jesus children'. In the light of the foregoing that is no longer strange. According to Steiner, these two Jesus children became one during the scene in the temple when they were twelve years old (Lk 2:41–52). The Solomon Jesus child, the Messiah-ben-David, died soon afterwards, while the Nathan Jesus child, the Messiah-ben-Joseph, grew in strength.[9]

The day of the Lord

In the genealogy in Luke, Joseph is mentioned (between Judah and Jonam, Lk 3:30), but he does not appear in the genealogy of Matthew. Who was this Joseph from whom the Messiah of Luke is descended? There is an echo here of Joseph, son of Jacob, who interpreted the Pharaoh's dreams in Egypt. Why him? Because he was his father Jacob's favourite. Jacob wrestled with the angel of YHWH and was thereafter called 'Israel' by him (Gen 32:28). 'Israel loved Joseph more than any other of his children' we are told in Genesis 37:3, which explains the title Messiah-ben-Joseph: the Messiah, son of Israel. In some esoteric Jewish circles, the suffering Messiah-ben-Joseph is viewed as the *tzadik,* the righteous teacher/redeemer. He is then also viewed as Adam Kadmon.[10]

From the Talmud quotations and other documents mentioned above, we have seen that the Messiah-ben-Joseph comes from Galilee; he is connected with the ten northern tribes of Israel. But the Messiah-ben-David comes from Jerusalem in Judah. The great ideal of the Jewish people was that the two kingdoms would be reunited. This would happen when the two Messiahs appeared, or became one. That was simultaneously to be the end of time, 'the day of YHWH' of which the prophet Malachi spoke. But before 'the great and terrible day of the Lord' came he would first send his prophet Elijah (Mal 4:5). The Jews are waiting for this day.

Conclusion

From the foregoing we may conclude that the first Jewish Christians based their Messianic expectations on the two Messianic expectations living in traditional Judaism. Physically, Jesus was descended from the Messiah-ben-Joseph and the Messiah-ben-David, as demonstrated by the two genealogies in Luke and Matthew. The Jews expected the suffering Messiah-ben-Joseph and the warrior Messiah-ben-David, the priest/prophet and the king. And it was their ideal that these two would become one: a priest-king. When the first Jewish Christians then claimed that this was the case in Jesus, the Jews could well go along with that.

However, according to the first Jewish Christians, the idea that Jesus was also the apocalyptic Son of Man (who was to suffer), was much more difficult to understand, as we have seen by the reaction of Peter. That idea lived more among esoteric Jewish groups such as the Essenes.

The pictures of the Messiah and the Son of Man stem from Judaism, but there is also a third image, namely that the pre-existent Son of God descended into Jesus at the baptism in the Jordan – as described in the New Testament – and that was even more difficult for the Jews to understand. But for the Greeks this was not a problem, because they were familiar with the idea of the Son of God as mystery image.

2
Mysteries and Initiation in the Greek World
Christine Gruwez

Among those who were going up to worship at the festival there were also some Greeks. They approached Philip ... and asked him, 'Sir, we should like to see Jesus.' ... And Jesus said to them, 'The hour has come for the Son of Man to be revealed in his spirit form. Yes, I tell you: Unless a grain of wheat dies when it falls into the earth, it remains as it is. But if it dies it bears much fruit.'

(John 12:20–24)

Two ways of understanding early Christianity

The appearance of the Christ was embedded not only in Jewish religion and culture with its Messianic expectations, as John van Schaik has shown, but also in Greek culture with all its philosophical riches and mystery wisdom. This Hellenistic culture is often called pagan, while the world of Peter, Paul and John and the early church is referred to as early Christianity.

Speaking about early Christianity evokes many questions, for this term encompasses the time before we can distinguish its first forms. In the first instance, it was a truth completely filled with life, a life that was at the same time the most absolute expression of truth. As living reality it revealed itself as immediate experience. Whoever participated in it had passed beyond words, beyond any conviction, for it had arisen and existed as an experience that touched the deepest core of people's inner life, and changed it forever.

Consequently, we need to recognise at least two aspects, each with its own influence and effect. On the one hand there is the historical aspect, which manifests in the form of facts in the dimension of space and time; on the other hand, we need to recognise that which transcends the historical aspect, which took place as a divine primal fact in the dimension of the spiritual. Without this divine primal event the historical circumstances remain fragmentary and meagre. But without the manifestation of the events in concrete time and place it loses its value and becomes irrelevant and sterile.

We also need to be able to see these two aspects in their mutual relationship, to recognise how a divine-spiritual being, who initiated this event, approached the realm of earth and entered it in such a way as to penetrate earthly reality and take it into itself. The incarnation of God's Son, his death and resurrection are then the pivotal deed, 'the Mystery of Golgotha.' This deed preceded everything that would later grow into institution and doctrine. As a mystery deed, as it was called by Rudolf Steiner, it formed the pivotal moment in the entire history of humanity and created a watershed of 'before' and 'after.' Not only humanity that was alive at that time, but all of humanity, past as well as future, are part of this event. This deed was accomplished on earth for each human being.

The Greek world

Christianity came into a highly developed world in which art, science and philosophy flourished to a level that was rarely equalled later, and where a well-structured society offered opportunities to a great diversity of peoples and cultures. Its wellspring was a new way of thinking which brought with it a high degree of consciousness of self. This type of thinking, which was characterised by a new, unprecedented clarity of concepts – and made it possible to think in dialogue with others – arose almost simultaneously in widely different places in the Greek world: in the school of Pythagoras in the south of Italy; along the coast of Asia Minor where thinkers like Heraclitus taught; in Athens where it reached its culmination in the figures of Plato and Aristotle. Like a sunrise, an incredibly vivid light of consciousness had risen in humanity.

The Greek world was not a particular territory; it was every place where Greek was the common language or, rather, the language of culture. The Greek language possessed exceptional plasticity,

2. MYSTERIES AND INITIATION IN THE GREEK WORLD

and could therefore express nuances that cannot always be readily translated. Latin did not have these possibilities, with the result that until late in the Roman Empire Greek remained the language of the intelligentsia. Moreover, in several philosophical schools a core concept was developed that would play an important role in the subsequent spread of Christianity: the concept of *Logos,* for which no other language offered an adequate translation.

This Greek culture, the most important element of which was its language and the thinking that was able to express itself in this language, was spread all over the Middle East by the conquests of Alexander the Great. Hellenistic culture – in which Greek and eastern elements mingled – became widely established, and the organisational talent of imperial Rome gave it a durability that would extend into the subsequent Byzantine Empire.

We may wonder what the sources were that permeated Greek culture in all its complexity and further developments with such vitality that there was an uninterrupted stream extending over a thousand years. For it lasted from the awakening of Greek thinking in the seventh to sixth centuries BC until AD 529 when, on Emperor Justinian's orders, the doors to the Academy of Plato in Athens were finally closed because the school was viewed as a threat to Christianity.

We may find an answer when we consider the mystery sites that lay spread over the entire Greek world. Initiations were enacted in these mystery centres and were to respond to human existential questions. Through the growing development of thinking, people lost their instinctive connection to the spirit and had to stand more and more on their own two feet. Many of these questions related to mortality and to the destiny of the soul after death. We can find an echo of these themes, which were increasingly prevalent in Greek society, in some of Plato's dialogues such as *Phaedo.* This dialogue is about Socrates and how, in the last hours before his death, he entered into conversation with his pupils about the mystery of dying, which he described as an initiation:

> Whoever arrives in Hades uninitiated and unaccomplished will lie in the mud, but the cleansed and perfected arriving there will dwell with the gods.[1]

He confirmed this at the actual moment of death by covering his face with a shroud just as during the initiation ritual the face of the candidate was covered by a veil.

Such existential questions led to a longing to fathom these most profound riddles of existence. As time went on, a vague expectation grew deep within Greek society, an expectation that was to find its fulfilment in the initiation event in the mystery centres. For, unlike the Jewish world, Greek culture had no prophets. In Judaism powerful figures of prophets time and again predicted the Messiah, and that led to a growing expectation. In the Greek world there were no such prophecies, but there was indeed an expectation. But this expectation had no name, it had no 'face,' at any rate not in the way it did in Judaism. At best we see a name emerging that actually emphasised its lack of form, namely the *agnostos theos,* the unknown god.

Although there were oracles with priests or priestesses, such as the Pythia in Delphi, the oracular pronouncements of these figures were made in a state of dulled consciousness. We know how the Pythia sat on a tripod placed above a cleft in the earth from which intoxicating vapours rose. Sibyls, as they were called in the Roman world, were not counterparts of the prophets. Frequently their pronouncements were a source of confusion, and only a wise person such as Socrates was capable of explaining these riddles.

Despite the radiance of the rising sun of Greek thinking, around the time of the Mystery of Golgotha there was growing a mood of doubt and lassitude. It seemed as if life was fading from nature, as well as from human inner life. It was as if a shadow fell over the light of thinking, in spite of the fact that this thinking soared higher and higher, especially in the further development of the Academy of Plato and other schools that grew out of it.

Plutarch tells a story of how a message was called out from a ship sailing along the coast, 'The great god Pan is dead!'[2] Pan was the god who represented the life forces in nature and human beings. But also within the mysteries the living transformative power was no longer working as strongly as before. The places were still there; the pilgrims, the ones who wanted to be initiated, continued to flock to them, but the divine powers were retreating and left the people in a state of confusion and despair.

Those were the conditions in which gnostic movements began

to form, beginning in the third century BC. They were all teachings of salvation, opening paths to self-redemption. Where the mysteries left off, human beings had to take their spiritual destiny in hand themselves.

The schools of the Stoics can similarly be understood out of this experience of a darkening in the mystery centres. In the Stoa, the world and the human being were interpreted in terms of a rational order in which, by inner training and insight into its divine guidance, human beings were able to maintain a state of balance. Here also, human beings had to take and maintain a position of their own and had only their own forces to fall back on.

Priestess in the mysteries of Eleusis with the holy basket on her head, the cista mystica, *holding the consecrated bread. Found in the inner court of the lesser Propylaea at Eleusis.*

Mystery centres in the Greek world

What was it that took place in a mystery centre? What is initiation? The Greek world had famous mystery centres to which people came from the ends of the world. They were on the island of Samothrace, in Ephesus (on the west coast of Asia Minor), in Eleusis and Delphi, just to mention a few. Their great number indicates the degree to which Greek culture was permeated and formed by these initiation centres.

The importance of these places was reflected in the myths which hint at initiation experiences. Thus the sun hero Heracles, who had to descend into the underworld and fetch its guardian dog, Cerberus, first had to undergo initiation. He had first to bring to birth in himself the core of immortality – which was the ultimate goal of initiation – so that, invulnerable in this core, he would be able to endure the terrors of the underworld. The *Odyssey* also presents pictures of initiation, for instance, when Odysseus had to withstand the songs of the Sirens, and later when he also had to descend into the underworld.

Every mystery centre was consecrated to a different god or goddess, and therefore they naturally showed differences in the elements of their ritual. The goal of the actual initiation was to bring about an inner birth. This meant that in the one who underwent the initiation – provided one had prepared for it in the right way – a transformation took place. A new vital element, that was not available before, came to light and became active. That was initiation. It was not simply a matter of gaining knowledge or wisdom while remaining essentially the same person. Initiation meant that one became a different person. Through the essential change brought about in initiation one became more oneself. A new element was born in initiates that enabled them to develop something which they would have been unable to develop simply out of their own nature.

This was the great theme of Greek initiation practice. No matter how hard human beings tried to lead good lives, how virtuous they were, how intent on study and learning about the world, no matter how they practised and exercised, all this asceticism did not mean that they could develop that part of their being that could only be developed in the mysteries. *Askesis* – our word 'asceticism' is derived from it – was only the necessary preparation for the initiation event. It was immortal core of their being that was developed in the mysteries.

A number of philosophers have written about mystery centres, albeit often in veiled terms. The best known example is Plato, who, in the words of Socrates, described the initiation process in a famous passage in the *Symposium,* where Socrates describes how he was initiated by Diotima. But Aristotle also visited mystery centres, including Samothrace. Plato, too, was familiar with many mystery centres in the Greece and in Egypt.

However, the best known documents are those of the biographer Plutarch, who lived in the first and second centuries after Christ and performed the function of priest in Delphi, the mystery centre dedicated to Apollo. In one of these documents, *On the 'E' at Delphi,* he gave a detailed description of the practices of both the worship service of Apollo and the initiation there. He also gave an extensive interpretation of the mysterious letter 'E' that hung at the entrance of the temple.

We may imagine that it was within these mystery centres that the concept of the *Logos* was developed, not only as a concept in thinking, but also as a living reality. Because Greek was such a wide-spread language, this word was for a great many people a living concept at the time when the *Logos* came to the earth and lived among humanity. No one needed to search for the meaning of this word; it had been prepared in Greek culture, it had a content and came from a language spoken by a great number of people.

Demeter and Persephone

For many centuries, the mystery site of Eleusis – today a dusty, dreary ruin situated between a cement factory and the off-ramps of a couple of expressways – was one of the most important places in the Greek world. Dionysus was worshipped there, but most of all Demeter. Her name Demeter *(De-* or *Ge-meter)* indicates the great Earth Mother, the same as Natura (the personification of Mother Nature) in the medieval School of Chartres. She is the one who creates the possibility for life to take on form on earth, for the human soul-spirit being to live in a body, for life forces to work in matter.

PART I: PRE-CHRISTIAN STREAMS

The initiate is called by Demeter. Detail of a terracotta relief in Eleusis.

Eleusis is about ten miles from Athens, and a sacred way connected the two. Twice a year holy festivals were celebrated: the lesser mysteries in Agrai, close to Athens, in February; and the great mysteries in Eleusis in September. Only those who had previously participated in the lesser mysteries, during which, like the first act in a drama, the abduction of Demeter's daughter Persephone was enacted, could participate in the great mysteries. After a nine-day fast a big procession would start from the Eleusinion, a temple at the foot of the Acropolis in Athens, and toward evening it would reach the gates of the Telesterion, the sanctuary in Eleusis. Only the candidates for initiation were allowed to follow the torch bearer into the forecourt. There stood the 'smileless stone' on which Demeter once sat.

Demeter grieved for her daughter Persephone, who was called the *Kore* (the maiden) in the mystery of Eleusis. *Kore* is the virginal aspect of the soul. Persephone was young and had not yet been touched by the realities of the created world. She was the picture of a very young soul hardly arrived on earth. She was abducted by Hades, god-king of the underworld. The myth, which was part of the mysteries, tells that Demeter searched unceasingly over the fields and hills, rocks and mountains, and through rivers and streams. The people heard the rumble of her feet on the earth as she looked for her daughter. When she realised that Persephone was no longer on the earth, she sat down on the 'smileless stone' and grieved.

There she was found by the daughters of King Celeus who reigned over Eleusis. Demeter assumed the form of an old woman and offered her services to the king's household and became the nurse of Celeus' youngest child. Because she wanted to bestow immortality on this child, she put it into a fire every night, a ritual in which she was caught one evening by the mother. Still grieving, Demeter had to leave the court of Celeus. By the aid of the gods of the upper world, however, an arrangement was made that enabled Persephone to spend two thirds of the year with her mother and the other third in the underworld.

This is an indication of the mystery of incarnation of the human being. In the underworld we are incarnated. Thereafter we sojourn in the world of life forces until we incarnate again. Thus as human beings we always alternate between existence on earth and existence in a sphere that is not material.

The lesser mysteries

The lesser mysteries took place every year, the greater ones originally once every four or five years – six months after the most recent lesser mysteries. But as the Greek world was darkening over time, the greater mysteries also took place more often, as if people were hoping to be able to achieve something by having them more frequently.

Several writers described the sacred procession. One of these is the author of comedies, Aristophanes (*c.* 445 – *c.* 388 BC), who described the procession that went from Athens in the direction of Agrai or Eleusis along the sacred way. It was a wild scene – no austere and silent event. The procession took place during the night and was accompanied by torch bearers. There were also maenads or bacchantes, priestesses of the cult of Dionysus, who ran around in a frenzied ecstatic state incoherently shouting. All kinds of shrill musical instruments and drums accompanied the procession. The people chanted one sole word, 'Iacchus!' Iacchus is the mystery name of Dionysus.

What took place in the lesser mysteries? As soon as one entered the mystery site, complete silence had to be observed. The torches were extinguished before entering the gate of the temple area where the initiation halls were. In the dark of the night, ritual purification rites were enacted. One laid aside one's own clothes and received a white cloth. The principal part of the lesser mysteries was the performance of a mystery drama.

These dramas did not present lofty, divine scenes. What was shown was the abduction of Persephone and the brutal violence with which she was dragged into the underworld and, against her will, made the spouse of the king of the underworld. The drama showed the extreme grief of Demeter who, when she could not find her daughter, became the nurse of the little prince, and how Demeter laid this child each night into the flames of the hearth. From the descriptions we know how this was staged. Between the spectators sitting along the walls of a rectangular hall and the place where this scene was enacted, stood a large basin with fire. The flames and the smoke obscured what was happening. But the most impressive thing was the thunderclaps that sounded during the scene.

The people watching this were shaken to the core of their being. Through this traumatic experience their soul was momentarily purified and loosened, so that for a moment they no longer knew where they were and what they did in life, loosening all bonds with their former state. This was the purpose of the lesser mysteries.

In his *Poetica* Aristotle wrote about drama and how it developed from the mysteries and had the purpose of purifying the human being. We can only be purified if the soul swings between compassion and sympathy on the one hand, and abhorrence and fear on the other. It is a movement in which the soul opens and enters into the spirit of another, and then swings to the opposite extreme of closing itself off in disgust and fear. In this shaking back and forth, for a moment the soul loses all its attachments and habit patterns. That was the goal.

Those who had gone through the mystery received a purple headband. Many who had participated in the mysteries in the same year came together annually to talk about the experience they had shared as a group, despite each having come just for himself or herself. In Eleusis anyone – man, woman, free or slave – could go through the lesser mystery. This was not the case for the greater mysteries.

The greater mysteries

The greater mysteries consisted of two essential acts, two great moments: the offering and the moment of initiation when inner transformation was achieved. Here also, an episode of the great drama was performed, namely the grief of Demeter and the return of Persephone from the underworld. This was a kind of prelude that served to introduce the essential acts.

There are images of Demeter that show her with something like a great hat, but this is a sacred basket with loaves of sacrificial bread. She stands there in her priestly attire; she is the divinity who receives the people. In the first part of the mystery acts, the basket was taken from the sacred shrine and placed in the centre; everyone then received a loaf of bread from the hierophant. People also received a fermented drink thought to be prepared from barley. Bread and drink were shared and any leftovers of the bread were put back in the basket, which was then returned to the shrine. This was a ritual act.

Then something remarkable happened. Two words were spoken, respectively 'let it rain' and 'let it grow'. When the people spoke, 'let it rain', they looked up and invoked the Father of Heaven. When speaking, 'let it grow', they looked down and invoked the Earth Mother. This formed part of the ritual act that took place during the night, like many other rituals. At the end of the night, when the sun rose and the hierophant had taken his seat on the throne that faced east, a cover in the roof was opened so that the rays of morning light could stream into the hall. This signified the end of the first part of the greater mysteries.

There was an interval, probably of several days, before the second part was enacted. This included the moment when the neophyte, the one being initiated, was able to 'behold the godhead'. The Greek word for this is *epopteia* (from *epoptēs,* initiate). It was not a vision. Everything that had been awakened enabled the neophyte to experience the divine presence through and behind the acts. In this second part Demeter was shown, as well as Persephone. There could also be two columns, one male and one female: the Heavenly Father and the Earth Mother. But the essential experience was that behind these columns the figure of a woman appeared with a child in her arms: the Iacchus child. Witnessing this, the spirit principle was awakened in the neophytes, provided they had prepared themselves correctly.

What did it actually mean to awaken the spiritual core in a human being who went through initiation? Let us compare the mysteries of Delphi, which Plutarch described extensively with those in Eleusis. In Delphi the preparations were the same as those described for Eleusis, but the great theme of the Apollo mysteries was *Know thyself.* In the last part, when the actual initiation took place, some of the neophytes were taken out of the circle to a separate room. The whole body, including the head, was wrapped in a white cloth like a burial cloth, as if to indicate that the 'old human being' died during the initiation.

What did the neophytes experience in this moment? Everything that had happened before was a letting go of the old human being, but the new human being was not yet there, because the initiation had not yet been completed. It was a moment in which they lost themselves, a kind of break in consciousness, like a moment of dying. Everything that had so far been part of their consciousness had melted away during the preparatory steps.

In that moment the hierophant in Delphi spoke the words, 'Thou art.' The neophyte replied, 'I am.' Sometimes the words came in the reverse sequence: the neophyte then replied, 'Thou art,' to the hierophant's words, 'I am.' The words became a kind of interaction. But what was really taking place was that in this moment the 'I am' became manifest in the neophyte. In that moment, the 'I', the spirit child or spirit principle, was born in the candidate.

In this birth, Dionysus had an important part as the child Iacchus, the child of the future, the spirit core of the human being. Dionysus could appear in three different guises.

As cosmic Dionysus he was called Dionysus Zagreus – similar to the name of the Zagros mountains in the North of Greece. The cosmic Dionysus was the spiritual being who carried in himself all the cosmic forces that could ever be individualised by human beings. However, these forces had not yet been taken into human beings at that time. It was the greatest that a godhead could encompass, but it was not yet humanised. In the myth as it was told in the mysteries, Dionysus Zagreus sacrificed himself. Showing the motif of dismemberment, he was torn apart into countless little elements. It was a sacrifice. Only then could the cosmic forces enter human beings. Dionysus let his own inner essence be torn apart so that out of all these little elements something new could descend into human beings which the human beings themselves could begin to develop. This was the first guise of Dionysus.

The second guise is the one we know best. It is the Dionysus who was the son of the supreme god Zeus and an earthly mother with the name of the moon, Semele. He was half god, half human. In this form he could appear as a faun or in the company of Pan with his procession, which represented for the Greeks the living nature forces as they work in created nature. Pan marched through the forests with his followers, and the lonely wanderer who tried to find his way out of the wood would hear his flute and, attracted by the melody, would then lose his way even more. At some moment he would then see the crowd of bacchantes and Dionysus himself. In this guise, Dionysus taught humanity the arts of viticulture and agriculture. As a demigod he brought them wine and bread.

Finally, there is the child Iacchus that came into being from the union of Dionysus, the demigod, with a divine being, as a result of which Dionysus made another sacrifice. The child was given to Athena, the goddess of wisdom, who took it under her protection and brought it up. That was the end of the myth, leaving the future open. It was this child that was shown in the greater mysteries.

We should not imagine the world of the Greek mysteries as one that was never spoken of. Everywhere it was known what took place in the temple spaces. An initiate was not allowed to talk about what was inwardly experienced there. What happened on entering the greater mysteries and what was achieved in the initiation, were things the initiate was never to mention. However, toward the end of the existence of the mystery schools this oath of secrecy was sometimes violated.

The mystery of the *Logos*

There are early Christian philosophers in the Greek world who knew the mysteries. Clement of Alexandria was one of them; another was Hippolytus, a martyr from the third century in Italy. They came from two different directions within Christianity as it was then developing, but they both knew the mysteries. Clement often referred to what took place in the mysteries but added, 'What I proclaim, to which I invite you, are the mysteries of the *Logos*.' This indicates that, for those who belonged to the Greek world, Christianity, as regards the elements of its liturgy and initiation (mystagogy), was a direct continuation of what was enacted in the mystery centres.

But there was also a big difference. The *Logos,* the spirit core that in the Greek mysteries was awakened in human beings in the moment of initiation, was awakened in such a way that, in a certain sense, the soul was then saved. Plato and many others had already stated that the soul is not condemned to wander in the realm of the shades in the underworld. For if the spirit core was awakened (as shown in *Phaedo),* one could sojourn in the company of the gods. But what happened with the body? This was a question that was not asked in the Greek mysteries. The body did not share in what took place during initiation. It had to wait outside, as it were; it did not participate in the initiation.

And of course an even bigger difference – and this would in the early centuries cause countless different movements and schisms within developing Christianity – is that Christianity proclaimed that the *Logos* became human and dwelt among us, as told by the Gospel of John. Every educated person in the Greek world could understand the *Logos* as the principle in the divine world that is shared by human beings, but does not become human itself. The *Logos* always remained part of the divine world and did not come to earth – on the contrary, human beings had to raise themselves from the earth, had to leave the earthly world of the senses.

The Christians who spoke of the *Logos* said that human beings did not need to ascend to the *Logos*, for instance by undergoing initiation in the mysteries. Rather, it was the other way around: the *Logos* was descended to the world of human beings, and had become human. For many prominent Greek people this was utterly incomprehensible.

When Clement of Alexandria said, 'As Christians we celebrate the mysteries of the *Logos*,' someone in his immediate circle would have understood it to mean that he thought that human beings would develop in such a way that they would ascend to the *Logos*. But what Clement meant was that humanity would develop so that it would be capable of receiving and encountering the *Logos* in and among themselves here and now. These are two diametrically opposite views.

The Greek world and early Christianity

The Greek world was crucial for the development of Christianity, if only because of the Greek language. Without this language the Gospel of John could not have been written. Its prologue could not have found expression in any other language. Even if we assumed that it originated in another language or had gone through a different development, the way the Gospel of John works upon the soul is directly related to the way the Greek language works upon the soul. It was at that time possible to experience the *life* of a concept through this language. In Latin this was no longer possible, because it was a language that served the development of the law. This required that concepts were very precisely defined. In Latin there are clear concepts, but life has withdrawn from them. In Greek concept and life are still united. The use of Greek or Latin later led to a crucial difference in the development of Christianity.

The Orthodox churches retained Greek, while the Western church went in another direction. The Easter festival in the Greek Orthodox church retains something coming directly from the Greek initiation mysteries of 2000 years ago. At midnight during Easter night – the lights are off, it is the dark – there is a knock on the door, the door is opened and suddenly there is light everywhere. This comes out of the tradition of the mystery acts of the pre-Christian Greek world.

We can see how Paul was able to express his Christ-experience and proclaim it to the world, thanks to concepts he could employ in Greek. This would have been impossible in Latin. Earliest Christianity was not so much expressed in what was said, but in that which worked *through* the words. The words made it possible for life to move back and forth among human beings.

However, where people were unable to have an inner experience of the descent of the *Logos* into the human world, we see increasing signs of degeneration in the wisdom of the mysteries. Many of the Gnostic movements are nothing but a degeneration of the Greek mysteries, which once brought such light and life to a large part of humanity.

A tragic figure in this regard is Emperor Julian the Apostate, who came to power after Constantine and his sons. Christianity had become the state religion which meant, on the one hand, that Christians were no longer persecuted, but also that the mystery character of Christianity gradually came to an end. Christianity became a religion. In a religion a godhead is worshipped in a temple or holy building, offerings are made to the godhead, prayers are offered to the godhead, a community directs itself to the godhead and together listens to readings from holy scripture. All these are elements of a religion. From the time when Christianity became the state religion, it became progressively more difficult to experience its mystery aspects. It was diverted from this mystery nature and led onto a different course. This was true especially and most clearly in western, Latin Christianity. By the ninth century nothing was left of any mystery nature. The mystics and the heretical movements, all of which actually wanted to return to the mystery aspects of Christianity, had not yet appeared – they had yet to develop. The Eastern churches went through a different development in this regard.

Julian the Apostate wanted to bring back the mystery in Christianity. He felt that this aspect was disappearing. He still sought the cosmic being of the sun as it was worshipped in pre-Christian mysteries, such as in the time of Zarathustra in Persia. Julian sought the divine being who had descended to the earth in the cosmic being of the sun where he no longer was. In his move to preserve the mystery character in Christianity he went in the wrong direction, back to what had worked in the past. Whether this was the cause of his tragic death aged 32 – according to some historians he was murdered by one of his bodyguards – remains an open question. But that he had understood what was happening in Christianity is beyond doubt. He too represented the picture of the Greek world into which Christianity was entering.

Summary

Taken together, the developments outlined above can be characterised as follows. In the Greek world there was a great expectation, but an expectation that was slowly oppressing minds. In the initiation practices in the mysteries something appeared that linked to this expectation. The first Christians in this Greek world viewed Christianity as a continuation of the mysteries, with the understanding that the *Logos* had become a human being and had lived upon earth. Those who did not enter into the stream of Christianity lived in a kind of longing because they could no longer find their real task. Some forms of Gnosis manifested a kind of despair and fear.

The western world, as well as Christianity, is inconceivable without the Greek world, for in and through the Greek spirit Christianity found a channel to reach the world.

The Gospel of John, describing the entry into Jerusalem, reports that there were many strangers in town, including Greeks. Christ spoke to them the words,

> Unless a grain of wheat dies when it falls into the earth, it remains as it is. But if it dies, it bears much fruit (Jn 12:24).

The Greeks knew this image from the Eleusinian mysteries. Before the bread from the sacred basket was distributed, in front of all those who were to participate in the meal, the wheat was ground by the priests. First the stalk had been cut with a sickle. In many pictures we see Demeter, but also the child she laid on the hearth, shown with an ear of wheat. The ear of wheat was an essential part of the ritual. The words of Christ to a little group of Greeks thus give much food for thought. They might be a reminder of the mystery of Eleusis.

3
Messianic Expectation and the Essenes
Bastiaan Baan

This was not at all in accord with the universal love of humanity felt by Jesus of Nazareth. It was unbearable to him that spiritual treasure should not be available to the whole of humanity but could only be gained by some, at the cost of humanity as a whole.

Rudolf Steiner[1]

The sources of Christianity were not abundantly flowing at the time when Jesus of Nazareth appeared. Christine Gruwez has described the dramatic moment shortly after the time of Christ, when along the coast of Greece the proclamation could be heard, 'The great god Pan is dead!' The Greek mysteries declared that the end of a road had been reached.

The Jewish sources of Christianity were apparently also exhausted at that time. True, there were all kinds of Messianic expectations, but how could it be that when Jesus appeared among human beings, he was not recognised as the Messiah in spite of all those expectations? On the contrary, he was ignored, mocked and opposed. These are indications that the sources no longer flowed in their original purity. This is also true for the third of the great precursors: alongside the traditional Jewish and Greek (pagan) cultures, the coming of the Messiah was also prepared by the Essenes, who did not act openly, but worked in secrecy.

Until about the middle of the twentieth century, not much more was known about the Essenes than a few scattered quotations from contemporaries between 200 BC to AD 70. After the destruction of the temple in AD 70, nothing more is written of them. Until recently, these contemporary descriptions were useless to most historians. There were indeed documents, but there were no archeological discoveries to prove that the Essenes ever existed. So their existence was doubted for centuries. One of the great researchers into the Essenes in the twentieth century even spoke of 'Essene phobia'. Because this group was so elusive and because there were so few statements by contemporaries, historians and scientists kept their distance. This changed in 1947, when the greatest archeological find of all time (as it was then called) was made: the discovery of the Dead Sea Scrolls.

I will begin with old documents and quotations on the Essenes from contemporaries. A second section contains the descriptions Rudolf Steiner gave of this group, especially in the year 1910. Finally, I will describe the finds of the Dead Sea Scrolls, which brought historical reality to light.

The old documents

One of the oldest reports on the Essenes can be found in Philo of Alexandria's (*c.* 20 BC – AD 50) writing *About the Contemplative Life*. Philo described in detail who the Essenes were, how they arranged their lives and where they lived. It is a lively and fairly concrete description of this little-known sect. Philo said that they lived not only in Judea, but were spread in small colonies over several places around the Holy Land including Egypt where they called themselves *Therapeutae*. Philo said that this was not because they were healers in the physical sense, but because they healed the soul.

Philo wrote about how they worked and acted, describing, for instance, that before the Essenes entered the order, they had to give up all their possessions. If they wanted to gather wisdom, they had to relinquish outer riches. In most of the Essene orders the person had to leave behind his family, city, possessions and land, and had to go into a place of seclusion. From the moment he joined as a novice, he led a life of prayer, singing or reciting hymns, exercises and physical discipline. Six days a week he read old scripture.

On the seventh day the Essenes discussed their reading in a special, cultured style. Philo seemed to describe his own observations that the eldest – we would call him the abbot – gave a speech 'which differed from that of the demagogues of our country.'

> And he, indeed, follows a slower method of instruction, dwelling on and lingering over his explanations with repetitions, in order to imprint his conceptions deep in the minds of his hearers, for as the understanding of his hearers is not able to keep up with the interpretation of one who goes on fluently, without stopping to take breath, it gets behind-hand, and fails to comprehend what is said; but the hearers, fixing their eyes and attention upon the speaker, remain in one and the same position listening attentively, indicating their attention and comprehension by their nods and looks, and the praise which they are inclined to bestow on the speaker by the cheerfulness and gentle manner in which they follow him with their eyes and with the fore-finger of the right hand.[2]

How different is this from our culture! We want to state immediately what we think of something. That did not happen in those circles; instead, they entered into the points of view of those who had acquired insight.

The nights were often devoted to hymns and songs of praise to the godhead. Because the Essenes did not use wine or other intoxicating substances, Philo was particularly struck by the fact that by singing songs of praise they came into a state of a kind of 'sober intoxication': an exalted condition in which they celebrated the godhead. At the end of the night they were sober and lucid again; for they rose at sunrise and sang with outstretched arms to the rising sun, after which they retired to their cells again. Philo gave the following description:

> The end [purpose] of ideas, and expressions, and chorus-singers, was piety; therefore, being intoxicated all night till the morning with this beautiful intoxication, without feeling their heads heavy or closing their eyes for sleep, but being even more awake than when they came to the feast, as to their eyes and their whole bodies, and standing there till morning, when they saw the sun rising they raised their hands to heaven, imploring tranquillity and truth, and acuteness of understanding. And after their prayers they each retired to their own separate abodes,

with the intention of again practising the usual philosophy to which they had been wont to devote themselves.³

It looked to Philo as if these monks 'lived on air' – his own words!⁴ Bread, water and salt formed the usual meals. There were also ritual meals at which bread and *tirosh* was served, an unfermented wine, which was probably also used during the Last Supper. The Essenes had no slaves; they also did not take food that had blood. In brief, in every respect we are reminded of strict monastic communities. It is an archetype or prototype of a monastic community. This was such a strong picture that in the Middle Ages people went a step farther, seeing in Philo's description the beginning of Christian monasteries and the Essenes as the first Christians. Even some academics fell into this trap, surmising that the Essenes were the first Christians. But later discoveries point to a pre-Christian community that was waiting for the coming of the Messiah.

We find a second, even more detailed description in the works of Pliny the Elder (23–79 AD), a Roman historian. He reported that the Essenes had a centre on the west shore of the Dead Sea near Ein Gedi, which many scholars identify with Qumran. It is hard to believe that it was possible for a monastic community to develop in this place. Actually, it is inconceivable; it is probably impossible to find a spot more dead than this one. The Judean desert borders the Dead Sea, which is so dead that any fish that swims from the River Jordan into the Dead Sea immediately dies. Close to the shore of the Dead Sea, in a desolate area with steep cliffs, the remnants of an Essene monastic community are hidden. After the discovery of the scrolls, excavations in the 1950s found the ruins of the monastery with spaces for common use, cells, tables and benches, gigantic cisterns and baths which can only be assumed were for ritual purification. But it remains hardly conceivable that a human community could flourish in such a spot.

The confusion around the Essenes existed long before the discoveries of Qumran, and when we read about the latest finds it only becomes worse. In the Middle Ages and in the Age of Enlightenment all kinds of things were mixed up with each other. It was known that the Essenes had something to do with the Nazirites, who dedicated themselves to the Lord making a vow to refrain from all intoxicating drink, cutting their hair, or becoming ritually impure by contact with corpses (Num 6:2). John the Baptist in the desert, as well as Jesus of Nazareth, were presumed to have had contact with the Essenes. For instance, Frederick the Great, the Prussian king during the Enlightenment, wrote in a letter to the French philosopher d'Alembert, 'Jesus was really an Essene'. This showed how in the course of history the distinctions between Nazirites and Essenes, or even between John the Baptist and Jesus of Nazareth, became obscure.

Statements by Rudolf Steiner

Long before the discoveries at Qumran, this tangle was unravelled by Rudolf Steiner in the lectures he gave on the Gospel of St Matthew in September 1910. In these lectures he made it clear that established academics wanted nothing to do with the Essenes, because they considered this group to be a legend. But, said Steiner, Christianity was prepared by the Essenes, who formed the most important messianic community at the time of Christ. The phrase 'messianic community' resonated, for I had come across a similar term used by one of the scholars of the Dead Sea Scrolls, who said, 'The Essenes were a Messianic elite in the desert'.

Steiner indicated what the significance of the Essenes was:

> These were the teachings needed for understanding the Christ's appearance on Earth, and they appeared first and most effectively among the Therapeutae and the Essenes.[5]

We would not understand Christ if there had been no Essenes. The Essenes, through their messianic expectations (we can ask ourselves where these came from), had a sense for the Messiah, and indeed recognised him in Jesus of Nazareth.

Rudolf Steiner went back to the beginning and said that the Essenes, long before they became a historical movement, were prepared when Moses instigated the order of the *Nazir,* those dedicated to God. They led an ascetic life and prepared themselves in small communities for the coming of the Messiah. The Essenes continued this tradition of the Nazirites, but more radically and strictly. In some places they took Isaiah's prophecy literally, 'In the wilderness prepare the way of the Lord' (Is 40:3), and went into the desert. We can find this quotation from Isaiah in the rules of the order in Qumran.

The term *Nazir,* which Rudolf Steiner used, also occurs in the scrolls of the order of Qumran. The community is there referred to as the *Nazir.* In the Roll of Hymns we find the expression 'We are the Nazir'. A similar word occurs in the well-known prophecy by Isaiah (11:1): 'There shall come forth a shoot [*nazr*] from the stump of Jesse'. It is an eloquent picture of the tree that was cut down, the trunk seemingly doomed to death, and from this apparently dead trunk a *nazr,* or new shoot, would sprout. The Essenes said: We are that new shoot. We are the small group that prepares for the coming of the Messiah so that the trunk of Jesse may bloom.

It is not only from the Essenes that we know the term *Nazir.* Matthew quotes Isaiah when, after the flight into Egypt and the massacre of the innocents, the family returned and went to Nazareth in Galilee, stating 'He is predestined to be a Nazarene' (Mt 2:23).

Historical documents sometimes contained contradictory reports on the Essenes. Was it really an exclusive, radical order? Were they also active in Nazareth? Did they just exist as monks in the desert? Did not entire families live in Nazareth? Rudolf Steiner explained these contradictions in the aforementioned lectures when he spoke about five streams in the order of the Essenes.

Around 100 BC the great teacher of the Essenes, Yeshu-ben-Pandira, appeared. He is mentioned in the Talmud. He spread the teaching of the Essenes to five followers, who separated in five directions and founded their own orders in several places in Palestine. Rudolf Steiner also called these five men by name: Mathai, Nakai, Netzer (cf. Nazareth), Boni and Thona; five disciples who each founded their own school with its own nature.[6] This indication by Rudolf Steiner makes it understandable why classical authors wrote such different things about the Essenes. For instance, the Jewish historian Josephus described that the Essenes lived in villages spread throughout Palestine (instead of in a monastic community in the desert), and that they came together in lay fraternities. In monastic terms, one could speak of a 'third order' that lived in small colonies in villages. In this way, Netzer founded the little town of Nazareth, where the old Nazirite practices were cultivated.

3. MESSIANIC EXPECTATION AND THE ESSENES

In addition, Rudolf Steiner described the inner path of the Essenes in a context that showed what was common to all five streams. The Essenes practised the inner path. In all circumstances – also when they lived in the 'third order' in a family – the inner path was developed: the inward way of initiation, the way into the 'desert', not only in an outer sense but also inwardly. The Greek word *eremosis* means both 'desert' and 'loneliness'. It indicates an outer as well as an inner condition (the word 'hermit' is derived from it).

After a night that was partly wakeful, an Essene would awaken slowly, remaining for a long time on the borderline between sleeping and waking, before coming to full wakefulness and perception. (There is an echo of this in the tradition of farmers who, after awaking, remained in bed for some time with the curtains closed, to muse on what had taken place during the night and what the day would bring). This habit was especially cultivated by the Essenes. By consistently practising the inward path, they developed a strong self, or 'I'. John the Baptist was an example of this: he lived for a long time as an Essene in the desert. All the descriptions of the Nazirites applied to him. One could speak of an 'I' that is condensed, made more solid on the inward path.

But, if practised in a one-sided and exclusive manner, this path can also turn into a dangerous trap. When a person wholly concentrates on the 'I', there is in the end nothing left but his own ego. They are then so self-involved that they no longer notice what else is going on in the world. This was certainly true for the radical order of Qumran. It developed into an almost fanatical order that turned away from the 'evil world' and – this was both its strength and its weakness – exclusively concentrated on the coming Messiah. There is something tragic about such an order if the rest of the world is shut off to such an extent that it no longer counts. Their focus and 'I' became separated from the surrounding world and its needs. The wellspring ran dry.

This takes us back to the beginning of this chapter, where I indicated that the two streams that flowed into Christianity, the Jewish Messianic expectation and the Greek mystery culture, had in a certain sense come to their end at the time of Christ. And so also this third stream. Here follows an example of the radical nature of the rules of the order of Qumran. The neophyte had to commit:

[to] seek God with a whole heart and soul, and do what is good and right before Him as He commanded by the hand of Moses and all His servants the Prophets; that they may love all that He has chosen and hate all that He has rejected; that they may abstain from all evil and hold fast to all good ... and may live perfectly before Him in accordance with all that has been revealed concerning their appointed times, and that they may love all the sons of light, each according to his lot in God's design, and hate all the sons of darkness, each according to his guilt in God's vengeance.[7]

A more radical black-and-white picture of the world is hard to conceive. That is the reason why an exceptional 'visitor' – Rudolf Steiner described how Jesus, when he was in his twenties, visited the Essenes and became acquainted with the order – recognised that the well had run dry. Jesus saw that this community had literally shut out evil, keeping it outside their gates, and in so doing allowed evil to work more intensively in the rest of humanity. The development of the members of this community was at the expense of the rest of the world.

The tragedy of a community that consistently does this for some centuries is that it shuts itself up in an ivory tower and keeps humanity out. Jesus recognised this after he had also recognised the tragedy of the Greek mysteries and that of the traditional Jewish orders. These insights developed for him into an incentive to chose a radically different direction: 'Love your enemies!' This was his answer to the Essenes. Jesus recognised the dead-end road, and he knew that there is no other way than connecting with evil, unconditionally and with the best intentions.

The Dead Sea Scrolls

In 1946 or 1947 a shepherd boy made a sensational discovery at Khirbet Qumran. The boy was missing one of his goats and climbed up along a rock by the Dead Sea. He saw a cave quite high up which couldn't easily be reached; it requires a steep climb. He threw a pebble into the cave and heard the sound of an earthen vessel breaking into pieces. He found – in the semi-darkness they looked like faces – a whole row of jars. It is easy to visualise that, in the total silence of the desert, he was scared to death. He realised that this was something incredibly old, hidden away perhaps for hundreds or thousands of years. He was like an intruder. He ran away. Only later did he tell one of his friends what he had found. They took courage and climbed up again and made a discovery of which they had scant idea of the import. Of course they were hoping to find coins, but instead they found rags and written scrolls.

The boy took one of the scrolls and showed it to an antique dealer in Bethlehem. Eventually it reached a scholar in Jerusalem who recognised it as the prophecy of Isaiah, but in a manuscript that was very much older than what had been known to-date.

Then begins the story we can read like a detective novel: how the scrolls went from hand to hand, the cajoling, the horse-trading, and the disappearance of the scrolls – until in the 1970s the media started demanding to know why these scrolls had remained a secret. Why was nothing ever published about them? Then followed a flood of publicity, from the sensationalised press to reputable scientific journals.

The Isaiah scroll was gradually deciphered, and it turned out that this manuscript was a thousand years older than the then oldest known text. And what no one had expected, the text of this scroll agrees almost word for word with the Isaiah prophecy as we know it from the Old Testament. It contradicted what many Bible critics claimed, that as the story was passed from mouth to mouth it would not take long before it was totally changed. And this scroll showed practically no change at all! A hundred years of Bible criticism and questioning of what is original and what was added later, was wiped off the table, as it were. It had always been presumed that the Bible was like a quilt of old and new fragments, but here was a coherent text handed down whole and complete.

Later discoveries in and around Qumran gave additional information on the views of the Essenes. It was an enormous library with writings about the origin of the world, the rules of the order, and the temple. The Temple Scroll describes all the functions and actions that had were to be performed in the temple – they differ from what actually took place in the temple in Jesus' time. We find several Messianic expectations and a little Apocalypse describing a final battle.

The scrolls show that it was not only a community that lived in expectation of the Messiah, but it also lived intensively in the expectation of the New Jerusalem. There are scrolls that describe the New Jerusalem down to the smallest detail as we read of it in the Book of Revelation – the measures of the city, the twelve gates, the precious stones. The Essenes of Qumran lived in the expectation of a new heaven and a new earth preceded by an Apocalypse, a final battle.

In several Qumran scrolls we find the explicit prophecy of a priestly Messiah and a kingly Messiah. They speak of two Messiahs who are to come. When scholars read this, their first reaction was: that cannot be, it has to be a copying error, for what did not fit their preconceived notions could not exist, or was explained away as a mistake.

It took some time before the scholars realised that they could not get around the problem. The scrolls tell very clearly of the expectation of a Messiah from the priestly line of descent (the lineage of Levi) and a Messiah from the royal line of descent (the lineage of David). The Essenes of Qumran lived with these expectations.

This perhaps makes it easier to understand Rudolf Steiner who, long before these texts were discovered, said that in this order of Essenes the knowledge of the coming of the Messiah was alive. This was a group that not only lived in silent expectation, but knew who would come and indeed also recognised him.

What the New Testament presents in images, the Qumran scrolls put into words and clear concepts. Jesus' message to his disciples 'You have the gift of being able to understand the mysteries of the Kingdom of God' (Lk 8:10) was something that pre-eminently applied to the order of the Essenes.

Besides the description of the two Messiahs, a third designation of the Messiah also occurs repeatedly in the writings of the Essenes, namely the Son of Man. However, they also used this term for themselves, calling themselves 'Sons of Man'.

Finally, I want to mention a statement by Rudolf Steiner that is not about the past but, remarkably, about the task of the Essenes in terms of our own time. Only once, in a lecture in 1910, did Rudolf Steiner describe this community not in its historical significance, but in terms of an actual current task:

3. MESSIANIC EXPECTATION AND THE ESSENES

> ... the most profound fact of modern history ... [is] that, whenever we deepen our spiritual life, we renew the Essene wisdom.[8]

Surprisingly enough, something ancient and seemingly forgotten appears to be the most timely task for us: the renewal of the wisdom of the Essenes.

I understand Steiner's words as follows. When Jesus was on earth there were hardly any human beings who knew who he was, who understood him and recognised him as he was in all reality. Humanly we may well imagine that someone with such a great consciousness had to suffer immensely when no one recognised him. We find this tragedy described in the Gospels. It is expressed in radical terms when Jesus announces his future suffering. In ever more explicit words, he prepared his disciples for this in three prophecies of suffering, but they did not understand what he was trying to tell them. In the last prophecy this inability is radically expressed with the words, 'But they understood nothing. His words were hidden from them; they did not grasp their meaning' (Lk 18:34). This is a very important part of the suffering of Christ. He does not just want to be understood with the intellect; he wants to be comprehended in the full sense of the word, with all human capacities. This is the task that relates to the renewal of the wisdom of the Essenes, 'the most profound fact of modern history'.

In 1910, the same year as Steiner gave his lectures on the Gospel of Matthew, he also began a series of lectures, titled *The Reappearance of Christ in the Etheric,* which revolved around the Second Coming or the *Parousia.* He said that, beginning in the year 1910, people will increasingly have some experience of the Second Coming. Just as Christ had once appeared in a physical body, he will in our time manifest in the realm of life forces, the etheric world. Anticipating the future, Steiner described in drastic terms what would happen if human beings do not recognise him and if they have not prepared themselves for this. He pointed especially to the 1930s. Again and again, Steiner reiterated that it is our task to be prepared so that we will be able to recognise the phenomena of the Second Coming. There is no doubt that what he called 'the renewal of the wisdom of the Essenes' is related to the proclamation of the Second Coming that has to be prepared for.

In this lecture series Steiner described that there would be people who would have experiences of the Second Coming, but would fail to understand them. He even said that it would be possible that people would end up in an institution if what they actually experienced was not recognised. Here again, comprehension is the critical factor. History repeats itself. When Jesus lived on earth there were but a few who recognised him as the Messiah. Now that Christ is to appear in a spiritual form, will there again be human beings who recognise him, or will he pass by unseen?

PART II

The Three Great Apostles

4
Peter, the Builder of Churches
John van Schaik

He said, 'And who do you say that I am?' Then Simon Peter answered, 'You are the Christ, the Son of the living God.' And Jesus said, 'Blessed are you, Simon, son of Jona; you have not received this revelation from the world of the senses but from the world of my Father in the heavens.'

(Matthew 16:15–17)

Greeks and Hebrews

Of the three apostles, Peter most strongly represented the classical Judaism of the Torah. He was most deeply imbued with the old soul forces in which the Father God revealed himself. In older theology, Peter was therefore viewed as the true apostle of the Father God. He belonged to the first group of Jews who became Christians but also wanted to remain faithful to Jewish tradition. Peter invoked the God of the patriarchs:

> Moses said: 'The Lord God will make a prophet like me come forth from among your brothers. Hear him in everything that he shall speak to you. Those souls, however, who do not listen to his word shall be torn from their people and given over to destruction (Acts 3: 22f, quoting Deut 18:15–19).

It is perfectly clear: Jesus was the promised Messiah-prophet. Based on that conviction many Jews converted to Christianity – they were familiar with the picture of the Messiah-prophet. Another typically Jewish concept is that according to Peter, Christ came to lead 'all existence back to its origins' (Acts 3:21). He came to restore the covenant of YHWH with his people. This required that one live fully in accordance with the Jewish laws and customs, including circumcision.

Circumcision as the sign of the covenant between God and his people was the first conflict within the original Christian community in Jerusalem. The conflict began in the community in Antioch, where Paul was reproached for converting pagans who were not circumcised. He was called to Jerusalem, where 'some who, from being Pharisees had become Christians' argued that pagans had to be circumcised, but Peter supported Paul (Acts 15:1–19).

After many more journeys, Paul again came to Jerusalem. James the Lesser, who is called the Righteous, was there but Peter had disappeared. Again, Paul was reproached for teaching Jews to be unfaithful to the law and the customs because he did not insist on circumcision (Acts 21:15–26). That Paul did not insist on circumcision is one thing; Peter had already spoken in favour of that. But that Jewish Christians no longer needed to observe the law – that went too far. Thus Paul became known in history as the apostle to the pagans, in other words the apostle to the Greeks, while the Jewish Christians of the first community were called the Hebrews. Among the very first Christians, there already arose a conflict between the Hebrews and the Greeks (Acts 6:1):

> In these days the number of disciples grew rapidly, and indignation arose among the Greek-speaking against the Hebraic members.

Peter: 1. Founder of the church in Rome

At some point in Acts, Peter disappears as the leader of the original community in Jerusalem. James is left as the only leader. Where did Peter go? Paul tells us that Peter lived for a time in Antioch, Syria, just as he himself did. In Antioch, Paul accused Peter of a wavering attitude in regard to the conflict about following Jewish law:

> For before some of those who were of the circle around James came there, he had sat at table with non-Jews; but when they

came, he withdrew and kept himself apart because he was afraid of those strict upholders of the circumcision. The rest of the Jews joined in his hypocrisy, so that ultimately Barnabas, too, was drawn into it. (Gal 2:12f).

When Peter had to choose, he evidently chose Jewish tradition. Even Barnabas, the close collaborator of Paul, proved to be receptive to the Jewish approach of early Christianity.

According to Paul, Peter must also have lived in Corinth (1 Cor 1:12, 3:22). There is no mention in the New Testament that Peter was ever in Rome, but it was presumed to be the case among Christians toward the end of the first century. In a letter from Clement, Bishop of Rome, we read that both Peter and Paul were in Rome. Irenaeus wrote at the end of the second century that Peter and Paul founded the church in Rome. But it is especially the apocryphal *Acts of Peter* that tell us about Peter in Rome. The *Acts of Peter* were written in the second half of the second century. The principal theme in this apocryphal document is the (spiritual) battle of Peter with Simon the Magician (Simon the Sorcerer). Peter won of course, for he invoked the Lord, while Simon invoked magic. This book describes how Peter incurred the wrath of wealthy Romans because he preached sexual abstinence. Marriages were disrupted and Rome was all stirred up. When Peter wanted to escape he met the Lord at the city gate:

> And as he went forth of the city, he saw the Lord entering into Rome. And when he saw him, he said: Lord, whither goest thou thus? And the Lord said unto him: I go into Rome to be crucified. And Peter said unto him: Lord, art thou (being) crucified again? He said unto him: Yea, Peter, I am (being) crucified again. And Peter came to himself: and having beheld the Lord ascending up into heaven, he returned to Rome, rejoicing, and glorifying the Lord, for that he said: I am being crucified: that which was about to befall Peter.[1]

Peter went back, was arrested and, at his own request, crucified upside down.

In Catholic tradition, Peter and Paul founded the church in Rome; but especially Peter. This is justified based on Matthew 16:18f:

And I say to you: You are Peter, the Rock. On this rock I will build my congregation and the gates of the abyss shall not swallow it up. To you I will give the keys to the kingdom of the heavens. What you bind on the earth shall also be considered bound in the heavens, and what you loose on earth shall also be considered loosed in the heavens.

Based on these words of Jesus, the pope is the successor of Peter. In Rome Petrine Christianity became visible. Peter was the foundation of the church because he was the first to confess that Jesus is the Son of the living God. This confession of Peter immediately precedes the quotation from Matthew in which Peter is called the Rock:

And Jesus came to the district of Caesarea Philippi. There he asked his disciples, 'Who do men say that the Son of Man is?' They answered, 'Some say John the Baptist, others say Elijah, and yet others say Jeremiah or one of the other prophets.' He said, 'And who do you say that I am?' Then Simon Peter answered, 'You are the Christ, the Son of the living God.' And Jesus said, 'Blessed are you, Simon, son of Jona; you have not received this revelation from the world of the senses but from the world of my Father in the heavens. (Mt 16:13–17).

For an instant, Peter was conscious that Jesus was the Son of the living God, but this consciousness immediately died again when Jesus started predicting his own suffering. When Peter protested against this prediction of suffering, Jesus said to him, 'Leave me, power of Satan' (Mt 16:23).[2] Very briefly, consciousness of Christ awakened in Peter, but it died again right away. Later we don't read about Peter as speaking of Jesus Christ as the Son of God; instead he invoked the prophet-Messiah of the Jews.

But the fact that Rome – the western church – bases itself on this insight of Peter, is because it is the church of Peter *and* Paul. For in Paul this insight truly broke through in his Damascus experience. And that is because, as was said earlier, Paul stood in the Greek tradition, in which the idea of the Son of God was a known theme (see Chapter 5 on Paul by Christine Gruwez).

Peter: 2. Founder of the church in Antioch

Peter is not only viewed as the 'rock' of the church in Rome, he was also the founder of the church in Antioch, the Syriac Orthodox church, founded in AD 37. February 22 is the feast day of the See of Peter in Antioch, while January 18 is the feast day of the See of Peter in Rome.

Antioch was the capital of Syria, and after Rome and Alexandria the third most important city in the Roman empire. In Jesus' time there was a large Jewish community. Antioch is even viewed as the birthplace of Christianity. Chapter 11 in the Acts of the Apostles relates that after James the Lesser had been stoned to death in Jerusalem in AD 62, many Jewish Christians fled to Phoenicia, Cyprus and Antioch. A Jewish Christian community soon developed in Antioch: 'In Antioch, the disciples were called "Christians" for the first time' (Acts 11:26).

Initially, this Christian community was Greek oriented, and Paul preached there to non-Jews (Greeks). Not everyone appreciated that. New Jewish Christians arrived from Jerusalem; people whom Paul in Galatians called 'upholders of the circumcision', in whose opinion the Christian community in Antioch was not Jewish enough. As we have seen, Peter chose the Jewish side, and Paul lost. Thus, in the *Ecclesiastical History*, Eusebius (*c.* 260–340) calls Peter the first patriarch (bishop) of Antioch.

It is therefore not surprising that writings circulated in Antioch carrying Peter's name. The ninth patriarch Serapion of Antioch (191–211) mentioned an apocryphal *Gospel of Peter,* dated between AD 100 and 150. The fragment that survives begins with the capture of Jesus and ends with the women at the open tomb after the Resurrection. The most striking difference with the gospels in the New Testament is that on the cross Jesus does not say 'My God, my God, why hast thou forsaken me?' but 'My power, my power, thou hast forsaken me!'[3] The words 'My power' are typically Jewish.

This early Jewish Petrine Christianity was gradually superseded in the first century by the Christians who followed Paul. That was already the case with Ignatius of Antioch (bishop 70–107); not only that, but this Ignatius was also a disciple of John. Another church father, St Jerome (*c.* 347–420) called Ignatius a disciple of the apostle John, because he emphasised the working of the Holy Spirit. Ignatius of Antioch can therefore be viewed as a representative of Pauline-Johannine Christianity. This decisively coloured the Syriac Orthodox church. But despite this, Paul and John colour the Syriac Orthodox church, just as Rome bases itself on Peter as its first bishop.

We have now traced two forms of Petrine Christianity. In a formal sense at least, the Roman as well as the Syriac Orthodox church base themselves on Peter as their founder. Their content differs in 'colour': the church of Rome is Petrine and Pauline, while the Syriac Orthodox church is Pauline and Johannine.

The Church of the East

What happened to the Jewish Christianity of Peter after Pauline Christianity became dominant in Antioch? And exactly what sort of Christianity was this? Historical research of the past few decades has shown more and more convincingly that, besides the Syriac Orthodox church, there were for many centuries many different Jewish Christian groups. With the rise of Islam in the seventh century, these Christian groups more or less sank into oblivion. All these groups are often combined under the term Church of the East. The most important and best known of these is the Nestorian Church (of which more later).

These Jewish Christian groups left a large body of evangelical documents of their own, whose content deviates from the gospels of the Roman and Syriac Orthodox churches. They are:

- The *Gospel of the Nazarenes,* the *Gospel of the Ebionites* and the *Gospel of the Hebrews*
- The *Diatessaron* of Tatian
- The writings of Thomas: the *Letters of Jesus and Abgar,* the *Acts of Thomas* and the *Gospel of Thomas.*

These documents will give us insight into the Christology of the Church of the East. We will examine them in order to trace Petrine Christianity in the region.

The Gospels of the Nazarenes, Ebionites and Hebrews

The Gospel of the Nazarenes: St Jerome wrote in 392 that he received a Gospel of Matthew from the Nazarenes in Beroea, now Aleppo, Syria. That gospel was probably written in Aramaic (Syriac). Another church father, Epiphanius, related in his *Panarion* ('medicine chest') that the Nazarenes were a Jewish Christian group, and that they had a gospel of their own. Only a few fragments of this gospel have survived.

Fragments of the *Gospel of the Ebionites* can also be found in Eusebius' work, where it was described as a Jewish-Christian document. This gospel probably came into being in an isolated group of Jewish Christians to the east of the Jordan in the first or second century.

The *Gospel of the Hebrews* was mentioned by Clement and Origen. Apparently, Jewish Christians in Alexandria used this gospel. It greatly resembles the *Gospel of the Nazarenes;* it may even be the same.

All three of these gospels reject the virgin birth. Only at the baptism in the Jordan was Christ ready for his work. During the baptism he received the spirit that made him the true apostle who had been expected. At the baptism in the Jordan, Christ was *made* the Son by the spirit of the Lord. This view is called adoptionism. The church father Irenaeus reported in AD 180 that these Christians taught adoptionism.[4]

Consistent with the Jewish-Christian nature of this gospel, after his resurrection Jesus appeared first to James, the brother of the Lord. As the leader of the Jewish Christian community in Jerusalem, James was held in high regard.

These Jewish Christians rejected the authority of Paul. Their worship service closely resembled that in the synagogue, and in Syria they had the most influence. A Christian state arose in Edessa (now Urfa, Turkey) under King Abgar IX (176–213), the first Christian ruler. The apostle Thomas was held in high regard. After the invasion of the Arabs these Jewish Christians disappeared from view and they were only 'rediscovered' in the twentieth century.

The Ebionites and the Nazarenes only recognised one gospel: the Gospel of Matthew. The word Ebionite means 'the poor one'. This points to strict asceticism. They seem to have believed that Jesus, while the Messiah dwelt in his body from the baptism to shortly before his crucifixion, purged the law of Moses from all deviations. Therefore, they insisted on strict observance of the law. The Ebionites rejected the view of the pre-existent Son of God; Jesus was above all a human being.[5] The Nazarenes accepted Jesus as the Messiah, and followed Jewish law, including the circumcision.[6]

Besides the Ebionites, Nazarenes and Hebrews, there were other Jewish Christian groups in the greater Syrian region. One of them we know as the Elcesaites, for whom baptism rituals played an important role and for this reason they were called a 'Baptist sect'. There were other Baptist sects in the region, such as the Mandaeans, which continue to exist in the South of Iraq and are known in the Koran as the Sabians.

The prophet Mani (216–277) grew up in the Elcesaite sect which was founded by the Jewish 'prophet' Elchasai in Mesopotamia in the first half of the second century, and which recognised Jesus as the Messiah. This shows that in the middle of the second century there were already Christians deep in the Assyrian empire. We know of his life from the *Cologne Mani Codex* which was discovered in Upper Egypt in 1969. Mani turned away from these Jewish Christians and converted to Pauline Christianity. From a Jewish Christian he became a gnostic. Mani was familiar with the apocryphal books of the East, such as the Acts of Thomas and the Gospel of Thomas. These writings will be discussed later.

The Diatesseron

The Syriac Orthodox church uses the *Peshitta,* the translation of the Bible into Aramaic. The Jewish Christians principally used the *Diatesseron* (harmonisation of the gospels) of Tatian. The *Diatesseron* (the word means 'one from four') is a summary of the four gospels that was written by Tatian in Edessa around AD 170. Tatian said that he was born in Syria, went to Rome and there converted to Christianity. In 172 he returned to the East where he became an adherent of the Encratites, a severely ascetic Christian movement in Edessa. The *Diatesseron* was very popular and was translated into

Arabic and other languages. Our Christmas story, with the three kings *and* the shepherds, is in fact based on the *Diatesseron*.

There are a number of passages in the gospels which Tatian, as a strict Encratite, could not quite accept, so he changed them. One of them is the marriage at Cana. The master of the feast said there, 'Everyone usually serves the good wine first, and then, when the guests have drunk much, the poorer kind' (Jn 2:10). In his harmonisation Tatian turned it into: 'Everyone usually serves the good wine first, and then the poorer kind'. The words 'when the guests have drunk much' were left out. And that is the way it reads in the Arabic *Diatesseron*, and maybe therefore in the Koran. Drinking wine was not acceptable to Tatian. He used documents for his harmonisation that are not canonical, probably the three above-mentioned gospels of the Hebrews, Ebionites and Egyptians, but certainly, according to Quispel, also the Gospel of Thomas.[7]

The writings of Thomas

The correspondence between Abgar and Jesus. Edessa (today's Urfa in Turkey) was an important centre of early Jewish Christianity in Syria. In the first few centuries after Christ, Edessa was situated outside the borders of the Roman Empire. After the destruction of the temple in AD 70 Jews and Jewish Christians of course did not seek refuge within the Roman Empire, but went outside it, preferably to one of the many Jewish communities that existed in the East since the Babylonian exile. The language spoken there was not Greek but a Syrian form of Aramaic, usually called Syriac. Edessa lay exactly on the border between the Roman and Parthian empires; sometimes it was Roman, sometimes Parthian. After 250 it became a vassal state of Rome, and the influence of western Christianity greatly increased. Many Jews and Jewish Christians then fled even farther to the East into the Sasanian Empire. In 226 the Sassanids came to power in Mesopotamia, and in 639 Edessa was conquered by the Muslims.

How the first Jewish Christians ended up in Edessa is not known but there are legends that trace the origin of Christianity in Edessa directly back to the first Christian community in Jerusalem. One of these legends speaks of a correspondence between the Edessan King

Abgar and Jesus. This correspondence forms part of a document with the name of *Doctrine of Addai,* which was written sometime in the third century. Briefly summarised, this document tells how King Abgar V – who indeed reigned from AD 9 to 46 – heard of Jesus' miraculous healings in Israel. Because he was ill himself, he invited Jesus to come to Edessa. Of course, Jesus did not go, but he did send a letter:

> Blessed art thou that hast believed in me, not having seen me. For it is written concerning me that they that have seen me shall not believe in me, and that they that have not seen me shall believe and live. But concerning that which thou has written to me, to come unto thee; it must needs be that I fulfil all things for the which I was sent here, and after fulfilling them should then be taken up unto him that sent me. And when I am taken up, I will send thee one of my disciples, to heal thine affliction and give life to thee and them that are with thee.[8]

After the crucifixion, the apostle Thomas remembered this correspondence and sent Addai to Edessa. Addai healed the king, and the entire city was converted to Christianity. It probably did not literally happen this way, but it does indicate that the Jewish Christians in Edessa felt a strong relationship with the first community and that, besides Peter, the apostle Thomas was very important to them. Thomas was deeply revered in Edessa. With a great procession in the year 394, the (presumed) relics of Thomas were entombed in Edessa. And thus the emergence in the East of apocryphal documents carrying the name of Thomas is not surprising.

One of those documents was the *Acts of Thomas,* written in Syriac-Aramaic and dating back to the first half of the third century, shortly before the Romans conquered Edessa and the city came under the influence of Orthodox Christianity. This can be observed in the *Acts of Thomas,* because they were revised to purge them of unorthodox views. The *Acts of Thomas* are related to another apocryphal document, the *Acts of Peter,* which probably originates from the same region.

The document relates how Thomas travelled to India and died a martyr's death there. Edessa lay at the beginning (or end) of one of the silk roads that run through India into China. Jewish Christianity was exported from Edessa to India along the silk road. Even today, the liturgical language in the church in Kerala, India, continues to be Syriac, and these Christians are still called St Thomas Christians.

The name Thomas is an Aramaic word that means 'twin.' In the *Acts of Thomas,* Thomas is called Judas Thomas and is the twin brother of Jesus. Thomas and Jesus are interchangeable in this story. It is a remarkable story which relates that Thomas was sold by Jesus to a merchant from India. On the way to India he came to a kingdom where the daughter of the king was celebrating her marriage feast. Thomas had just blessed the bride and bridegroom, who then withdrew into the bridal chamber. The bridegroom opened the curtain to pull the bride toward him and saw Jesus sitting there having a conversation with the bride:

> And he saw the Lord Jesus bearing the likeness of Judas Thomas and speaking with the bride; even of him that but now had blessed them and gone out from them, the apostle; and he [said] unto him: [Didst] thou not [go] out in the sight of all? how then art thou found here? But the Lord said to him: I am not Judas which is also called Thomas but I am his brother.[9]

Christ then proceeded to instruct the married couple in the 'true' life and dissuaded them from consummating the marriage. It is one of the passages in the *Acts of Thomas* that indicates a strict ascetic orientation.

According to the Dutch scholar Gilles Quispel, the *Gospel of Thomas* originated from Judean Christians descended from the first community in Jerusalem. It was written around AD 140. These Jewish Christians had no need of the pagan Christians of Paul. The Greek influence on Jewish Christianity only became dominant in this region in the fifth century. It became a famous gospel and consists of 114 pronouncements made by Jesus. It begins as follows:

> These are the secret sayings that the living Jesus spoke and which Didymos Judas Thomas wrote down.[10]

One half of the 114 sayings have parallels in the New Testament, not according to the *Peshitta* but according to the *Diatesseron*. In the *Gospel of Thomas,* Christ is not the mediator by death and resurrection; he is merely the teacher who helps human beings to come to know their own true self. Self-knowledge leads to knowledge of God:

> When you come to know yourselves, then you will become known, and you will realise that it is you who are the sons of the living Father (3).

This is Jewish: Jesus is the prophet who points the way back to God, just as the Old Testament prophets did. The human being has to try to become like Adam again. This presumes that the human being has to strive to become androgynous, must become one again. It says, 'When you make the two one' (22). This means that the genuine Christian is celibate, which the *Gospel of Thomas* derived from Jewish esotericism, while the traditional rabbis concluded from such views that one has to be married.[11]

Be this as it may, the *Gospel of Thomas* demonstrates a very early Jewish form of Christianity. It contains no teaching of Jesus that goes against Judaism. Its orientation on Jerusalem is evident in verse 12, where the disciples of Jesus are told to follow James the Righteous after the death of Jesus; James was Jesus' brother and led the first community in Jerusalem. Jesus as Son of God or Son of Man does not appear in the entire gospel.

The Hymn of the Pearl

What do these documents tell us about Petrine Christianity in the Church of the East? First of all we miss the Greek dualistic sense of life of Paul. We miss the radical gap between God and humanity as experienced by the Greeks at the time of Christ. For that reason, the image of Christ as reconciler and redeemer is of less importance. Christ is described in terms of 'restoration' and 'renewal', just like the restoration of the Covenant in the Old Testament. The view is one of the human being drifting apart from God, rather than a (Greek) break. Creation is therefore not in travail, as Paul wrote (Rom 8:19f); it is not broken; the human being has drifted away from God. This means that the body – and the entire cosmos – do not need to be healed by Christ – again according to Paul (Col 1.3–5) – but human beings have to find the way back to Paradise.

Once, YHWH made a covenant with his people. Christ renewed this covenant in the individual, as had been presaged by Jeremiah:

> But this is the covenant which I will make with the house of Israel after those days, says the Lord: I will put my law within them, and I will write it upon their hearts (Jer 31:33).

The first Christians referred to that, for instance, in the Letter to the Hebrews in the New Testament. By his death Jesus renewed the old covenant. Now it was no longer a whole people that had to strive for a connection with the Father; each individual must strive for the restoration of the covenant.

The way toward restoration is magnificently described in the *Hymn of the Pearl,* which forms part of the *Acts of Thomas.* The hymn speaks of the son of a king who lives in heaven and goes down to the earth to fetch a pearl that is guarded by a dragon. When he comes to the earth he forgets his task, but his parents write him a letter from heaven that reminds him of his task. He starts on his way, conquers the pearl and goes back to heaven where he receives a radiant robe.

We can view this hymn as an allegory of the way walked by a Petrine Christian to find unity (the pearl). It can also be the way of Jesus that must be followed. In that picture, Jesus is not so much the redeemer but, rather, the 'example' of the way back to God. Christ reveals God's way of salvation because this way was revealed to him by the descent of the Holy Spirit, Wisdom, at the Baptism in the Jordan. In the Church of the East, Jesus was viewed as the suffering servant of God, the last prophet and the definitive interpreter of Jewish law.[12]

Adoptionism was taught more in the Church of the East than in the Roman or Syriac Orthodox churches. As we mentioned before, the Church of the East had a very hard time with the doctrine of the two natures of Christ. The view of the two natures – Christ is God *and* man – presumes a break between God and human being that is healed by Christ. Eastern Christianity is much less concerned with that than the west. In eastern Christianity the problem of the two natures of Jesus Christ developed in two opposite directions: the

Nestorians emphasised the humanity of Jesus, and the Monophysites taught that human nature merged into divine nature. In essence, the Jewish Christianity of Peter did not recognise the problem of the two natures.

The way back to original unity is the way back to Paradise, to God; in Aramaic: to Alaha. The word Alaha is related to the word Elohim from Genesis 1. Even today Arabic-speaking Christians use the word Allah for God. Allah is therefore not only the God of Islam. One of the meanings of Allah is Holy Unity, the All, the ultimate power or the ultimate potential, the One who has no opposite. That is the unity that needs to be restored. This unity not only exists in Alaha, it is to be found everywhere: in ourselves, in nature and naturally also in the divine. The human being has to become Adam again, a (whole) human being, 'Son of Man'. In Jesus this was brought to realisation, and thus the unity of Alaha was restored, and Jesus had *become* the Son of God: *Yeshua bar Alaha*.

Peter: 3. The Nestorian church

The most important stream in the Church of the East was the Nestorian church. In the year 424, the Patriarch of the Church of the East convened a meeting of its 37 bishops for the purpose of founding their 'own' church, because the Church of the East could not accept the emerging doctrine of the dual nature of Jesus Christ as was finalized a few years later in the Councils of Ephesus (in 431) and Chalcedon (in 451). The doctrine of the dual nature showed too great an influence of Paul for the Church of the East. The report of the Council of 424 began as follows:

> All of these bishops offered a petition to the chief, head, and leader of all the bishops of the East, the venerable of God and holy Mar Dadiso the catholicos. They asked of him that he return to his see and stand at the head of the church of God, ruling and leading the flock of Christ in all the lands of the East, which had been committed to him by Christ in the high priesthood which he had received, as (it had been committed) to the head of the apostles, Peter.

> ... He is our leader and caretaker, the giver of all the stores of the divine treasure, Mar Dadiso the catholicos, who is Peter for us, the head of our ecclesiastical council.[13]

Here we have Peter again. The Church of the East was also based on Peter, but without Paul. Peter without Paul results in a very different kind of Christianity. That becomes evident when we turn our attention to the man who gave his name to the Nestorian Church of the East. Nestorius (381–451) had a remarkable career. From his beginnings as a monk in a monastery in Antioch, he became the patriarch of the Byzantine church in Constantinople, comparable to the Pope in Rome, but finally he ended as a heretic. Patriarch Nestorius had an increasingly difficult time with the doctrine of the dual nature: Jesus Christ is man *and* God. This was the view that led the church to regard Mary as the Mother of God, *Theotokos*. Nestorius opposed this view. He said that in his human nature Jesus Christ was born from a human being.

Nestorius' view was not new. When around AD 200 Syrian church teachers took up the Greek *Logos* doctrine (Christ is the *Logos),* they did this differently from the way the western church took up the *Logos* doctrine. The Syrian church teachers spoke of a created *Logos,* while the western church spoke of the *Logos* as the pre-existent Son of God. The Syrians said that this raised the danger of two gods; for them the Father God is all-important. This is called Monarchianism, and in consequence the Trinity is rejected.

We are encountering conceptions here such as we can also find in the Koran. Mary did not give birth to the Son of God, she gave birth to an ordinary human being, who was at best adopted by God as his son at the baptism in the Jordan. Jesus was the greatest prophet. These kinds of views culminated in 318 with the Alexandrian presbyter Arius (256–336) when he rejected the incarnation doctrine. According to Arius, Jesus Christ was an ordinary creature, while western Christianity, led by Athanasius (bishop of Alexandria from 328) taught that the Son is of the same nature as the Father.

This was the famous *homoousion* of the Councils of Nicaea and Constantinople. 'Of one being with the Father' was not possible according to the Syrians, for they said that Christ was a human being, and could therefore never be 'of the same being' with God. Arius was therefore condemned as a heretic. Along the same line, Nestorius was later also condemned as a heretic at the Council of Ephesus in 431.

According to Nestorius, the *Logos* took possession of Jesus to the extent that he was obedient to the Father. Jesus Christ was not of one being with the Father but he had the same will as the Father. Nestorius' opponent was Cyril, another patriarch of Alexandria, who had the opposite point of view: Jesus was God from his birth and became more and more human. This is Monophysitism, as mentioned earlier.

Thus Nestorius taught that Jesus was human and became more and more divine through grace; Monophysitism taught that Jesus was God and became more and more human. In 451 the Chalcedonian Creed was formulated precisely between these two extremes: of one being in two natures. For the non-orthodox Syrian Christians this western formula (it came from the Roman church) was unintelligible. For them it had to be one or the other: Nestorian or Monophysitic. As mentioned before, the doctrine of the dual nature was never really understood in eastern Christianity, because the Greek Christology of Paul never really took root in the east. The Church of the East remained more within the tradition of Jewish Christianity.

Conclusions

Virtually all great churches view Peter as their founder. That is the case in Roman Christianity, Syriac Orthodox Christianity and the Church of the East. But in substance, these churches differ greatly from each other:

- The 'church of the west' in Rome is oriented on Peter and Paul;
- The Syriac Orthodox church is oriented on Paul and John;
- In the Church of the East, Paul is conspicuously absent and Thomas appears side by side with Peter. This results in a very different kind of Christianity.

We have established that, relative to Paul and John, Peter stood most clearly in the tradition of classical Judaism. He was the apostle of the Father God. We have been able to trace Petrine Christianity in the many Jewish-Christian groups that continued to exist in the Church of the East until the rise of Islam. By examining a number of apocryphal documents of the Church of the East we have found what form this Petrine Christianity adopted. Compared with Syriac Orthodox Christianity and Roman Christianity we are struck by the following:

- Jesus as the Messiah was viewed primarily as a prophet in the tradition of the Old Testament prophets. He was the last of the prophets.
- Jesus the Messiah was viewed as a human being of flesh and blood who was more and more inspired by God during his life, and became divine at the Baptism in the Jordan. He became increasingly 'of one will with the Father.'
- The image of Jesus as the pre-existent Son of the Father was generally lacking.
- The idea of redemption through reconciliation was generally lacking. Redemption in the Petrine Christianity of the Church of the East was expressed mostly in the restoration of the original unity with the Father. Due to Jesus, the covenant once made by YHWH with his people was now made with the individual.

From left to right: John, Peter, Mark, Paul. Albrecht Dürer, The Four Apostles, 1526, Alte Pinakothek, Munich.

5
Paul, in Whom Christ Lives
Christine Gruwez

He said to me: 'I am Jesus the Nazarene whom you are persecuting ... Rise and go into Damascus. There you will be told everything that has been ordained for you to do.'

(Acts 22:8–10)

Paul the 'apostle to the nations,' was a Hellenised Jew. Besides the many other things this might entail, it also meant that he used the Greek language. It was the language in which he thought, wrote and spoke, and perhaps also felt. Hellenised Jews had spread all over the Mediterranean world of the time. Philo of Alexandria (20 BC – AD 40), who was a contemporary of Paul and, just as he, came from a strict, orthodox Jewish family, wrote a brilliant doctrine of the *Logos* in Greek.

Paul's original name was Saul. He received the name Paul, which means *little,* during his first missionary journey after the event of Damascus. On the island of Cyprus the Roman proconsul Sergius Paulus summoned him to proclaim God's word at his court (Acts 13:7ff). Paul there exposed the magician Elymas. From that moment he was called Paul.

We first encounter him as Saul at the stoning of Stephen, where those participating in the execution of the sentence laid their garments at Paul's feet so as to assure that these would not be defiled (Acts 7:58). The depth of Saul's passion to destroy becomes visible here, and it is these same 'passionate hatred and destructive urges' (Acts 9:1) that drove him to Damascus.

PART II: THE THREE GREAT APOSTLES

The Saul-Paul enigma

Paul appears on the stage as an enigma. But isn't the same true for every apostle, every disciple, every individuality who appears at the tender beginnings of Christianity?

As regards Paul, we may perhaps look for the distinctive features of this enigma in the many contradictions he evokes. Paul leads us to extremely human questions, questions about human existence which occur to all of us in the course of our lives – questions relating to all kinds of hardship, hunger and thirst, exposure to the elements and to the arbitrariness of the powers on this earth. But also to questions about discord among people whom one would expect to be in harmony with each other, such as the way Paul and the apostles of the original Christian community in Jerusalem disagreed with each other more than once. He evokes in us what, in a human sense, lies closest to our personal experiences and which we all know forms part of our human existence. We encounter in him both the greatest and the least of what a human being can represent. But at the same time, Paul evokes questions that we can grasp to some extent, but the full depths of these questions and their answers are so huge and all-encompassing that we are no longer able to grasp them.

Such a moment, in which we receive a glimpse of the magnitude of the figure of Paul, can be found in one his most famous texts. It is from the First Letter to the Corinthians, which is not only familiar to us, but is something that we can actually experience:

> If I speak out of the Spirit with the tongues of men and of angels [but] if I am without love, then my speaking remains as sounding brass or tinkling cymbal (1 Cor 13:1).

It is such an intimate text that everyone can live into it and transform it into an inner experience. Then the potential arises of sharing in the strength of such certainty, of such a power of conviction, that his words open up and become an immediate experience. And when Paul wrote, 'If love is truly present it cannot be lost' (1 Cor 13:8), one can almost sense how in him love grew into a driving force. It is this love that was able to convert his passion to destroy into submission in service to a higher will; a higher will that is no longer his own, but with which he identified his own personal will.

This enabled him to undertake the great journeys that tested him and his companions to their limits. It was out of this power that he was able to open the hearts of his listeners, and that he performed his miracles. It is as if he no longer had any fear, no matter how often he had to run for his life. Ridicule and hatred did not touch him. The hatred of Christians, which he had overcome in himself, now faced him. And standing before figures of authority who called him to account, such as Proconsul Gallio, elder brother of Seneca, in Achaia, he fearlessly spoke out of this power, with the result that the complaint against him was declared invalid (Acts 18:12–16). People recognised that Paul not only proclaimed the living God, but participated himself in divine life with his entire being.

Paul before Damascus

The basis of a biography is formed by the dates of birth and death. In the case of Paul, we are totally in the dark in this regard. We have no certain dates either of his birth or his death. It is as if the course of his life took place in the open, without our being able to get to know it in detail. But actually, such particulars didn't really play a role in Paul's case. There was one all-important moment in his life, something that came to be of such essential significance that we can only say that whatever preceded it and whatever followed it, it was a life that moved toward this central event, and not a life that simply took its course between birth and death. Paul's life consisted of a before and an after the central event around which his entire biography revolved, namely what occurred to him before the gates of Damascus on his way from Jerusalem. In all probability this happened in the middle of his life; at any rate, it forms a pivotal midpoint.

If we try to discover signs that preceded this event and pointed to it – after all, we share in what developed out of it – we have to look with different eyes. If we look at what preceded this event, knowing that in a certain sense everything in Paul's life steered him to that particular moment in the middle of his life when he was in that particular place with that particular intention, then we may indeed recognise it as a conversion. But it is a conversion of such depth and with so many layers that the word 'conversion' falls short of truly representing what took place there.

We are able to establish that, in the first few years after the Mystery of Golgotha, people in many places converted to Christianity. But here also the word 'conversion' is not quite adequate to represent what really took place. It was much more a matter of an immediate opening of the heart, as the soul-spirit organ, than becoming convinced in response to any words or deeds. At any rate, why would the conversion of Paul – if strictly speaking it was a conversion – be of such universal significance? This does not diminish Paul's contemporaries who converted to Christianity, but it begs the question: can Paul's experience before Damascus tell us more than what we commonly understand under the concept of conversion? A conversion is in itself a grandiose event. Could it be even greater and work even more profoundly? How could we imagine that?

Paul born in Tarsus

Paul was born in Tarsus, a seaport in Asia Minor, now Turkey. This was a city that for a number of reasons was important. The Greco-Roman world of the time was a large area where Greek was spoken, where the culture was based on Hellenism, and the Roman element had brought order and structure. Tarsus was not as now an insignificant town, but at that time was a cosmopolitan sea port. In his important work, *Saint Paul,* Emil Bock pointed out how, in Paul's day, the philosophical schools in this city had developed the leading philosophy of the time: Stoicism, the philosophy of the Stoics. Stoicism is known for its ethics, the gist of which is that human beings can maintain their equilibrium between the impulses that work in on them both from outside and from inside. But the Stoics also developed a *logos* doctrine that explained the Stoic principle of self-maintenance by the effect of a *logos* principle that can become active in every human being. Seneca, who was a contemporary of Paul, is an example. There are apocryphal stories that Seneca and Paul knew each other but we have no proof of this. Seneca was no Christian; he was a Stoic and a teacher of the Emperor Nero.

Emil Bock also called attention to something that perhaps adds another element to the significance of Tarsus. It was where the philosopher Apollonius of Tyana (*c.* AD 2 – *c.* 98), a person whom we know through a whole range of writings, grew up and was educated. He had schooled himself in esoteric science, he practiced magic and could perform miracles. Some people say that if, at the time of Christ and Paul, someone of that area were asked 'Who is the most amazing, most impressive person you know?' the answer would have been 'Apollonius of Tyana'. Around Asia Minor and the Middle East he was known as a philosopher, a miracle worker, a healer and someone who rescued people from the personal distress in which many were then living.

From what Paul himself said, we know that he was born into a Jewish family – probably of the tribe of Benjamin, the youngest of the twelve progenitors of the people of Israel. The family followed the strict rules of the Pharisees, strictly and even fanatically adhering to the law as they understood it. Within the stream of the Pharisees the Messianic expectation was all-important. Remarkably, the Pharisees also existed in Hellenised regions. Its adherents probably no longer used the original Hebrew Bible texts, but the Greek translation called the Septuagint. Being part of Greek culture and yet faithful to the Jewish beliefs and the Messianic expectation were not mutually exclusive.

Paul, Jew and Pharisee

Paul, like his father, was a tent-maker. That was strange in Greek culture. Working with your hands and culture were contradictory: either you had culture and had other people working for you, or you worked with your hands and had no culture. However, it was one of the characteristics of the Pharisees and the tradition in which Paul grew up, that a person could on the one hand be highly educated and, on the other hand, earn his living by working with his hands. In his letters to the first congregations, who wanted to shower gifts on him, Paul repeatedly wrote, 'I do not accept anything from you; I can take care of myself'. Whatever he received in the way of gifts was given back to the congregation that gave it.

In all probability, during his three great journeys Paul would often have been sitting at a loom to weave the cloth that, in addition to leather, was used for tents. It is generally agreed that he dictated his letters, perhaps while sitting at a loom. An educated, cultured person did not write his own letters, he dictated them. At the time it was customary to speak what one wanted to write, and have someone else write it down. We know that John thus dictated the Book of Revelation. Though dictating while working at a loom was perhaps something that made Paul unique.

The Acts describe how Paul was questioned: 'Who are you really?' In the eyes of officials who were responsible for maintaining peace and quiet in their territories, his contradictory activities made him look like a troublemaker. We read in Acts:

> 'Do you speak Greek? Are you not the Egyptian, then, who recently stirred up a revolt and led four thousand murderers into the desert?' Paul replied: 'I am a Jew from Tarsus in Cilicia, a citizen of a respected town. I request permission from you to speak to the people.' (Acts 21:37–39).

These were the circumstances in which Paul was working. He had to bring his message among the people.

In the Acts we find brief biographical descriptions of Paul in which he always begins by saying, 'I am a Jew'. In one place he says 'I received my education at the feet of Gamaliel' (Acts 22:3). Gamaliel (d. AD 52) was a famous rabbi who lived in Jerusalem, and probably a grandson of the even more famous rabbi Hillel the Elder (*c.* 110 BC – AD 10).

Gamaliel is mentioned twice in the Acts of the Apostles. In Acts 5:34f we are told that Peter and John had to appear before the Sanhedrin because of an accusation of causing trouble – interesting that the accusations so often mention this:

> Then one of the Sanhedrin stood up, a Pharisee named Gamaliel, a teacher of the Law who was famous and popular with all the people. He ordered the men to be sent out for a short while. Then he said: 'Men of Israel, consider carefully what you are about to do with these men.'

Peter and John owed it to the intervention of this Gamaliel that they were not immediately exiled from Jerusalem.

When Paul said, 'I received my education at the feet of Gamaliel', he was in effect saying: 'I had a wise master; I received religious instruction that went far beyond memorising sacred texts.'

Gamaliel was known not only for giving explanations of the Torah, but also for going deeply into the text. There are no further indications as to what occurred between Paul and this teacher whom everyone knew to be a wise man full of compassion. But one thing is certain: the Messianic expectation, the expectation of the Anointed One, must time and again have been the central subject in Gamaliel's teaching.

The Messianic expectation

Paul encountered the teaching of the Messianic expectation at a very young age. We can try and sense what lived in people's souls if, from childhood on they continually lived in a kind of permanent expectation of something that was coming, and which they hoped and believed they would live to experience. They were continually poised for the next step; they did not look back, but were always focused on the future, when the Messiah would appear.

Reading the letters of Paul, we can get the impression that he was an incredibly impatient person. This impatience grew out of the keen expectation of something that was to happen, something that still lay in the future. Rudolf Steiner, and later Emil Bock, connected this with Paul's statement that he was 'born prematurely' or 'untimely born'.

In the First Letter to the Corinthians where the death and resurrection of Christ are mentioned for the first time (1 Cor 15:3–8), there is also another important statement – and to appreciate this we should realise that the letter was written before the gospels. Paul described that the risen Christ appeared first to Cephas, then to the twelve, and then to more than five hundred brothers at the same time. 'Last of all,' said Paul, 'he appeared to me also, who am one born prematurely.' A most remarkable statement.

In the course of the centuries, theologians have interpreted and discussed it, and it is quite possible that he was a premature child. One thing of course does not necessarily exclude another, but Rudolf Steiner and Emil Bock connected it with the keen expectation that was living in Paul as an ongoing inner condition. Those born prematurely have to catch up, as they were unable to complete something; they are always focused on something they want to make their own. That is one possible explanation. There is also another one, to which I will return later.

As we have seen, Paul appears for the first time in the Acts of the Apostles at the stoning of Stephen, the first Christian martyr. Although Paul (then still Saul) did not participate in the actual stoning, it is possible that he organised everything so that it could take place. There is one important detail in the description that can be interpreted in different ways. Those who were present at the stoning (be it to execute it or simply as spectators) took off their cloaks and laid them at Paul's feet. Did they do this to prevent defilement? In Jewish tradition it was also customary to take off one's cloak before the man in charge. Paul let this happen. We may perhaps understand this as the sign that the execution could begin. It is described as follows: 'And the witnesses laid down their garments at the feet of a young man named Saul' (Acts 7:58).

The story of the Stephen's death as a martyr describes the extremely dramatic but also profoundly moving sign in which in the last moments of his life the heavens opened and he saw a divine light. Although this is not expressed in Acts, we can sense that it did something to Paul. The darkness of his urge to destroy cannot but have been struck by this light of revelation.

Nevertheless, the next chapter in Acts begins with this one simple sentence: 'But Saul took pleasure in all that happened when they killed him' (Acts 8:1). The Greek text has the word *syneudokōn*. *Eudokeō* means 'to agree' and the preposition *syn* means 'together'. In other words, he fully agreed with it. Paul therefore had not a shadow of doubt that the deed in which he had participated was justified. The next passage emphasises this: 'On that same day a great persecution began against the congregation in Jerusalem ... Saul raged against the congregation' (Acts 8:1–3).

At the moment when the power of the risen Christ shone through

5. PAUL, IN WHOM CHRIST LIVES

Stephen, in Paul the will to destroy emerging Christianity was whipped up into a frenzy. It is one of the riddles of this figure. How could he, while still so young, watch a human being, as young or even younger than himself, be put to death in such a horrible manner? The next day the persecution of the Christians was intensified. What drives someone to do such a thing? The persecution increased. After it began in Jerusalem, Paul wanted to extend them over a much greater area, and, with the approval of the High Priest, he decided to go to Damascus. The High Priest gave him a letter authorising him to arrest anyone who proclaimed to be a Christian.

Noon before Damascus

Again we witness Paul's incredible drive: while the persecution in Jerusalem was still in full swing, he was on the way to Damascus. And there the event took place for which everything that preceded it was a strange kind of preparation. Paul arrived before the gate of Damascus, the gate that leads to the 'street called straight'. From historical documents we know exactly where that gate stood; a part of it can still be seen.

When he had arrived near the gate in the heat of the day it was noon. It is hard to avoid the impression that the external circumstances – it may indeed have been the middle of the day – expressed something far deeper. Midday is a very special moment when the power of the sun is at its height. In that moment Paul fell to the ground, not by the power of the sun – although it would not have been surprising if that had happened – but a tremendous light shone about him, a light that in his own words was 'brighter than the sun itself'. It was not the sun that brought him down. It was a light shining around him brighter than the sun at midday.

This event is described in three places in the Acts – in chapters 9, 22 and 26 (what I have described here is from chapter 26) – as if the event was so great that it had to be told three times. The first time one cannot yet grasp it; one has to hear it a second and a third time. The light that shone about Paul caused him to fall from his horse. Many sculptors have pictured this, sometimes in relief, on capitals of columns in cathedrals. Paul fell to the ground and heard a voice 'saying to me in Hebrew: "Saul, Saul, why do you persecute me?"' It is evident that this was no mere physical occurrence, during which Paul lost consciousness because he had been struck by the sun, because of the question that was being asked. Paul asked, 'Who are you, Lord?'

It has been pointed out that in this question Paul uses the Greek word *Kyrie* (which we know from *Kyrie eleison*). It is the Greek equivalent of the Hebrew *Adonai*. Paul was therefore not addressing a human being but was asking God directly. It was immediately clear to him from what realm the light was coming. He addressed the godhead he knew from Jewish tradition with the name that could be used: 'Adonai, who are you?' Then came the shattering answer: 'I am Jesus whom you are persecuting.'

In the third version of the story in Acts 26 the voice spoke again to Paul and said, 'Now arise and stand on your feet'. He was given a task:

> 'I have appeared to you to make you a servant and a witness to what you have seen and what I will reveal to you in the future. I shall make you free of your people and of all the non-Jewish people to whom I send you.'

It was the moment when Paul was called to be the 'apostle to the nations', a title he was often given.

Who are you, Lord?

We have to stop and consider a few things more closely in this pivotal, crucial event in Paul's life. First and foremost the voice that answered Paul's question, 'Who are you?' did not answer with, 'I am Christ', but, 'I am Jesus'. We could think that these two are the same, but Jesus and Christ are not identical. Christ is the Anointed One, the Messiah. For Paul, the Messiah was someone he expected and not someone he persecuted. He did not persecute Christ, he persecuted Jesus.

Who was Jesus? Jesus of Nazareth was the human being who presented himself in the Holy Land as the Messiah. At that time, Paul was persecuting a human being who was crucified and who, in the eyes of Paul, had declared of himself to be the Messiah. For that reason, the answer to Paul's question was exactly right: 'I am Jesus whom you are persecuting.' But we still have to consider this further. He was no longer able to persecute Jesus because Jesus had been crucified. In the eyes of Paul, Jesus was dead. Therefore, when the voice answered, 'I am Jesus whom you are persecuting', this could only mean, 'You are persecuting the one working in all those who become Christians'. Thus Jesus was not this one human figure, rather that which worked and lived in the growth of the first Christian communities. Ultimately this was the one who was persecuted by Paul, although until the event of Damascus Paul himself was not conscious of it.

Both Steiner and Bock say that in that moment Paul went on the path from Christ (the Messiah, the Anointed One) to Jesus. Paul then *comprehended,* but not in the sense that we understand something that was not clear to us before. Paul comprehended that the One he was awaiting and seeking stood before him, not only in his present form, but as the being of Christ who connected himself with Jesus of Nazareth in such a way that both went through death and resurrection. Paul comprehended that this was the being who appeared to him.

For the rest of his life Paul tried to live up to what he comprehended in that moment, but was not yet able to express in words. For that reason we should not view this as a conversion, rather as an initiation. It is an initiation in which the one who approached Paul entered into him and connected himself with him in such a way that Paul later said, 'It is not I who live, but Christ lives in me' (Gal 2:20).

Paul needed the rest of his life to bring to realisation what happened before Damascus. In that sense we can understand it as a conversion, a turn, a *metanoia,* a change in the very being of Paul himself. He shared in the light-being of Christ. The light-being which he viewed as outside at the stoning of Stephen, that whipped up his destructive urges, came to him in the event before Damascus. In that moment Paul came to a point where he could allow it to enter into himself. He was blind for a time. He was blind in the everyday sense but he also was blind in a different way that allowed him to remain living in the event so that it could work deeply into him. He had to hold it in himself for a time before he could look out into the external world again. He had to have darkness around him in order to allow the event to permeate into the depths of his soul.

He probably stayed in Damascus (or Arabia) for about three years before the moment came when he could begin his missionary journeys. That was the time it took for the event before Damascus to penetrate him so deeply that it could work out of his own being.

Initiation

In his book *Old and New Mysteries,* Bastiaan Baan described the event before Damascus as an initiation in which several steps may be distinguished. First there was something that presented itself as a light, something one beheld. Paul himself used the words 'heavenly vision' (Acts 26:19). One could say that this was the first step of what was enacted as an initiation. We know it as the stage of 'imagination'. But then it came closer and spoke; that is the stage of 'inspiration'. Something was spoken to Paul. And in the question he asked and the answer he received, we see the encounter of being with being: 'intuition' – that is the essential core of the initiation.

The initiation began when Paul had to surrender the power over himself: he fell from his horse. He became powerless. He could no longer direct himself, he lost control and he had to let go. After the initiation he received the task of becoming a witness, which means that he had to live out of the change that had taken place in his being – to live out of this, to work out of this and to speak out of this.

We need to mention a few other elements from Paul's life and work. During his life, something developed that could be called a Christology. That is not the same as a theology; his was a living Christology, for everything he proclaimed was first experienced by him. He did not speak about it and he did not discuss it; he spoke out of his own inner experience.

There is a difference between Paul and other apostles – and at times there was great tension between them. Paul is sometimes viewed as the thirteenth who joined the group of twelve that was reconstituted after the crucifixion. The apostles and the first disciples who had experienced Christ after Easter, and had been in Christ's immediate circle until Ascension, felt that this was a first phase in the return of Christ. The life and work of the group of apostles came out of that phase, which was concluded at Ascension. But this did not apply to Paul. In this regard it is true that he was born prematurely, for Paul's mission commenced when the second phase began to unfold. It was the phase in which the being of Christ began to expand into the etheric, the life realm of the earth and humanity, and gradually became one with it. Out of that realm Christ worked on the earth and humanity; in that realm he may be encountered and experienced. This was different from the experience of the other apostles. Paul was the one who experienced the second phase of the return of Christ.

The first phase lasted until Ascension and can be characterised as 'we in Christ'. But what Paul experienced was 'Christ in me'. It is an inversion from 'I in Christ' to 'Christ in me'. This difference alone may have been the cause of much mutual misunderstanding, certainly between Peter and Paul – although they are often pictured together, for instance by Dürer (see p. 78).

Regarding the Christology of Paul, we can highlight a few elements because they are important and characteristic of Paul. Peter and John also had personal relationships to the Christ-being; each one 'lived' Christ in his own way. For Paul the motif of the Son was key. For him, Christ is the Son. If there is a son there is also a father; Paul still used the Aramaic word *Abba* to address the Father. But for instance in the Letter to the Galatians (4:5f) he said, 'so that we might receive sonship' and 'Now that you have become sons'. Paul was someone who spoke in dynamic terms out of his own powerful experience. He did not say, 'we *are* sons of God' but 'we *receive* sonship' and 'we have *become* sons of God'. From servants we become sons through the sonship of Christ. And through the sonship of Christ we become heirs, just as Christ as the Son is also the Heir. We set out as servants, or slaves, but because Christ is the Son and intended to become the Son in the evolution of humanity, we are able to be born anew from servant, from bound human being (the Old Adam), into sons of God. If the power of Christ works in us, we become sons. This was the great message of Paul: we are called to freedom. We are not free. We are summoned to become free. Our freedom lies in our becoming sons because someone went before us in becoming a son, and this continues to grow in us.

Another aspect, which is to be found in the Second Letter to the Corinthians, and on which Paul also elaborated in other instances, is something that lived on in many Greek-oriented, Alexandrian church fathers. It is the idea of the image. In a unique way Paul attempted to explain the relationship between Father and Son and between the Son and the human being as follows. God is the archetypal image, but when God wants to make himself known to humanity, he does this as an image of his own archetypal image. And that is the Son. The Son is the image of God, who is the archetypal image. Here we see the incredibly close and intimate mutual relationship, for both need each other. But in his turn the image, the Son, is able to turn toward the human being. When this happens, he is no longer the image of God, but becomes himself the archetypal image, and the human being becomes the image. We can find God by turning toward this archetypal image, Christ, and beholding the countenance of God which is turned toward us. For we know that the countenance that God shows us is, in its turn, a mirror image of God – God who wished to observe humanity and in this way begat the Son.

It is a picture that mystics have taken up. It is a process in which the one who is both image and archetype – namely Christ as the countenance of God turned toward humanity – becomes transparent. Paul himself experienced this becoming transparent before Damascus. But it can be experienced by every human being. The moment the human being becomes transparent to the light of Christ's true being, Christ, as the countenance of God that is turned toward humanity, becomes transparent to God who shines through it.

My weakness is also my strength

The above reflections contemplate one aspect of Paul's Christology that has found its way into the development of the Christian philosophical schools in the eastern Mediterranean area. But there is another aspect of his Christology of which I have the feeling that it can still be developed further, because it relates so closely to our experience today. That is why it is so often said that Paul stands close to the modern human being. It is the dialectic between strength and weakness; a special subject that is unquestionably also related to the Damascus event.

Expressed in my words, Paul said: Christ can enter into me, not because I am so strong but because I am so weak. This is one of the greatest contrasts we come across in Paul, not once but repeatedly. It is my weakness that makes it possible for Christ to enter into me. What he means is the weakness which, in spite of our intention to do the good, makes us do evil, so that I catch myself all the time in my imperfection. This is what Paul calls weakness, powerlessness. Developing the ability to squarely face this powerlessness makes it possible that Christ can enter into us as strength. But this strength is not my own; it is Christ in me.

In one place Paul went so far as to say that for him the proof that Christ lives, that he is a living reality and not a wish or something he dreams or fantasises about, is that Christ works through him. The proof lies in what Paul indicated with these words, what I can achieve with my words can never come forth out of me. Therefore, there has to be another power which works through me, and which brings about what is described in the letters and in the Acts of the Apostles. Of one thing I am certain: this cannot come from him, the man Paul. For him this was proof of the reality that Christ lived in him. These are moments when we discover a very different aspect of Paul. We find it in his well known statement in the Letter to the Galatians (2:19f):

> But through the Law my higher self died to the Law, in order to live for the realm of God. I am crucified with Christ. So it is not I who live, but Christ lives in me.

The connection between weakness and strength can also be found in the Second Letter to the Corinthians (12:6, 9) where Paul said, 'It would by no means be foolish of me if I wanted to praise myself'. And he continued, 'I would rather praise myself for my weaknesses, so that the power of Christ can be with me'.

In *Old and New Mysteries,* Bastiaan Baan describes how many words Paul uses that begin with the prefix *syn*; this prefix always indicates *together with, connected with* (the Latin equivalent is *con*). Paul also gave the word conscience a clear content. This word, *syneidesis,* also begins with *syn*: that which enables us to see coherence and relationships that connect things with each other, is conscience (*con-science*). If we can only see our own part, our conscience is still asleep. It awakens when we recognise things in their mutual relationships. It is Paul's great theme proceeding from the event before Damascus.

In 2 Cor 12:7 we read the famous phrase 'a thorn has been given me in my physical body'. Paul said nothing about what it is – for ages people have speculated what it might have been. The point is that time and again he supplicated God to take this thorn away, because he lacked the strength to do so himself. But Christ said to him, 'Be content with the grace that flows to you from me. The higher power completes what is lacking in human weakness'. Our experiences, due to this weakness and the powerlessness it brings with it, is the situation in our time today. But this powerlessness creates the opening through which the power of Christ can become complete.

Paul, the apostle to the nations

At some point Paul crossed the Aegean Sea from Asia Minor to northern Greece, to proclaim his message in Europe. Paul's letters show a surprising equilibrium. Three were addressed to congregations in Asia Minor – Galatians, Ephesians, and Colossians – and four to Europe. He wrote to the Romans – by far the longest letter, which is said to contain a kind of Christology – then to Corinth and Philippi, the city where he first landed in Europe and where Lydia was the first person in Europe to convert to Christianity. And then there are the Letters to the Thessalonians, who were actually the first to receive a letter from him.

However, there is one great city to which he never wrote a letter, showing that there was no Christian congregation. In his letters, Paul mentioned communities that were not founded by him, such as Jerusalem where he would go several times to attend the synods that took place there. It is the city of Athens that had no Christian community founded either by him or by another disciple. How could it be that in this city, which at that time embodied the quintessence of cultural achievement, no Christian community came into being?

In Acts 17 we read of Paul's visit to Athens. When he arrived there he first did what he always did: he visited the synagogue and spoke to the Jews. He indicated that he was most easily understood by them because they expected the Messiah. He did not need to explain the

5. PAUL, IN WHOM CHRIST LIVES

Messiah. He had to proclaim that the Messiah had come for them and was alive, even though he was crucified, and that he was resurrected from death. He brought the message of the risen Christ.

After visiting the synagogues – there were many in Athens – he did what he usually did: he went to the *agora,* the marketplace where many people came together. Philosophers would spend their day on the *agora* in Athens, speaking to some and arguing with others. Paul mingled with them. What he had to proclaim was very strange. The Athenians, however, liked a bit of sensation, and liked to hear about strange things. Thus a number of philosophers said to him, 'Your words sound strange to our ears,' and they took him with them to the Areopagus, a prominent rock north of the Acropolis which functioned as the court for major crimes. On the Acropolis was the temple of Athena, the goddess of wisdom. She had founded the city with a sign: she made an olive branch grow out of the rock on which the temple was built. The olive tree was consecrated to her and was a sacred tree in these parts.

At the Areopagus, they asked him to explain his teaching. Paul went along with them. The Acts relates that in Athens 'his spirit was powerfully stirred'. It was not his soul but his spirit that was deeply moved.

The members of the Areopagus were assembled. Raphael has pictured this scene in a life-size sketch for a tapestry (see p. 96). We see Paul preaching to the wise men and one single woman, all dressed in philosophers' cloaks and looking at Paul with sceptical and proud faces. They felt superior – who was he, a provincial stray from Asia Minor, to think he could tell the Athenian philosophers something new? They were waiting for the cut and thrust of a battle of words.

Then Paul made his speech. He said, 'Athenians, I see that you are devoted to the gods in every respect'. That was a surprise to them. He also said why he began with these words. 'I have gone through your town and have looked at your shrines.' For a devout Jew like Paul, who did not allow images of God, it may have been a shock to see all those statues in Athens. Practically every square or street corner had a statue, not to mention all those around and in the temples. Paul went on, 'and I found an altar with the inscription: To the Unknown God'. Then came the statement that says everything. 'The one whom you revere, without knowing him, he it is whom I proclaim to you.'

93

PART II: THE THREE GREAT APOSTLES

Raphael, Paul preaching in Athens, cartoon for a tapestry, Victoria and Albert Museum, London

This had not been expected by the wise men. Paul then described the God who created heaven and earth, the human beings who belong to the earth, and all that lives between heaven and earth, and also that from the power of this god the dead will be raised to life again.

This must have been so bewildering to these wise men that many of them got up and left without a word. Others stayed to scoff but two people stood up and converted to Christianity: Dionysius and Damaris, the woman. Raphael pictured them in the foreground. They are watching Paul attentively. Damaris was the only woman who was allowed to be present in this council of wise men. There was a rule that only the leading priestess in the mystery of Eleusis could be a member of the Areopagus. The unknown god was the god experienced by Greeks initiated in the mysteries, although they had no name for him. In the words he spoke on the Areopagus, Paul made public what was an actual experience for initiates. 'The one whom you revere, without knowing him, he it is whom I proclaim to you.' Dionysius the Areopagite and Damaris, who were familiar with these mysteries, immediately recognised what Paul was alluding to; they were directly touched and stood by Paul.

In this light, we can understand that what developed in Athens was the first Christian esoteric school. Dionysius became the founder of Christian initiation as mystery school, which developed and continued to influence western Christianity until the ninth century. The figures who passed on this Christian mystery knowledge from generation to generation were always known as Dionysius the Areopagite. In the early sixth century, one of these also left documents attributed to Dionysius the Areopagite. This led to some confusion as scholars pointed out that it could not be the same person as had heard Paul speak, and hence call the author Pseudo-Dionysius.

6
John: The Imitation of Christ
Bastiaan Baan

He who lay at the breast of Jesus, to him God entrusts the greatest and most perfect words about Jesus.

Origen, Commentary on the Gospel of St John

John: a perfect human being

When we look for a person's own nature, if we look in the right way, we will always find something that is quite particular to them. It is precisely these particular characteristics which make a person interesting or irritating, attractive or repulsive; in other words, it is food for psychologists, psychiatrists and novelists, who all look at a person's own nature from a special angle. We can do this with the most diverse people; we can even apply it to certain saints.

Psychologists, psychiatrists and critics have made many efforts to characterise what is unique in the great saints Paul and Peter. That is not so difficult. Although Peter was called the 'rock,' a critical theologian once said, 'Instead of Peter (Rock) he should really have been called "Quicksand"'. That was one kind of weakness Peter had. The strength was there of course, but there was also something irresolute, something wavering in his nature. There are psychiatrists who have said of Paul's 'thorn in the flesh' (2 Cor 12:7), 'This man was no saint but an epileptic'. In brief, it is not so hard to haul a saint over the coals; there is almost always some tender spot with which we can bring them down.

However, when we consider John the Evangelist it appears to be impossible to find anything we could call questionable in his nature. No matter where we look or what we read in the works that were written about John – just as many works as were written about Paul and Peter – whether it is in the gospel, in the apocrypha, legends, or the works of the mystics, psychologists or theologians, we cannot find flaws. That is particular characteristic of John. He wrote, it seems, a perfect gospel, and he was, it seems, a perfect human being.

Jesus and John. Wood sculpture from Upper Swabia, c. 1320. Stiftung Preussischer Kulturbesitz, Berlin

I would like to make a comparison, although it really takes the above statement down a notch. Consider what happens when a more or less 'perfect' person accomplishes something great, let us say Raphael, or Leonardo da Vinci, or Mozart, who created works of art. These great ones, who achieved something brilliant in their works of art, are known for their capacity to create something new,

6. JOHN: THE IMITATION OF CHRIST

and for the fact that this new accomplishment makes the impression of being simple, so apparently simple that it speaks to everyone. It made a deep impression on me how in Communist times the Sistine Madonna, one of the most famous paintings by Raphael, was admired by the public in Dresden, East Germany. People came in a never-ending stream – housewives with their shopping bags, middle class and working class people, tourists, art lovers – and everyone, from whatever background, was attracted to this painting. It is characteristic of a great, exceptional work of art that in its apparent simplicity it speaks to every human being.

This is particularly, and even more convincingly, true for the Gospel of John than for any other work of art. Down into his use of language it can be demonstrated that this evangelist says much with a relatively limited vocabulary, in contrast to the three synoptics, Mark, Matthew and Luke, who formulate things differently. With relatively few words, John was able to express more than the three other gospels – and he did this in such a way that every human being can understand his words. A child can 'comprehend' the stories of John. It is nourishment for a childlike faith; but also for mystics, theologians, philosophers the John Gospel is an inexhaustible spring.

The unique position John occupied, both in an outer sense and his place in the circle of disciples, can easily be recognised and is eloquent testimony of his relationship with Jesus Christ. This position is indicated at the Last Supper. No other human being has ever been described as 'lying close to the breast of Jesus' (Jn 13:23). At all times, people of all ranks and positions, from the most childlike faith to the most highly developed theology, have recognised something exceptional in the fact that one human being occupied that place, literally and figuratively close to Jesus.

The relationship between Jesus and John

There is a concept that, as it were, opens the 'inside' of this relationship, and indicates that there existed an exceptional affection between Jesus and John, an exceptional connection. This is *agapē*, the Greek expression for the highest form of love, the love Jesus had for John, an expression that was used exclusively for this disciple, 'the disciple whom Jesus loved.' The word *agapē* was not used for any of the other disciples. However, it was used for the connection of Jesus with Lazarus and his two sisters.

The Gospel, the legends and apocrypha have different ways of expressing this exceptional relationship of *agapē*. For instance, Voragine's medieval collection, *The Golden Legend,* relates that Jesus and John met for the first time more than three years before the Baptism in the Jordan, when they were both about 27 years old. The legend tells that Lazarus, a rich young man, one of wealthiest men in Palestine, invited Jesus to his house and hospitably looked after him. From this first meeting, confidential conversations developed between Jesus and this rich young man, and within a short time this relationship reached such depth and strength that when Jesus entered the house he embraced Lazarus. What happened that Jesus took a person into his love to such an extent that he embraced him?

From the Gospel we know what could occur from a single touch by Jesus, not only by the touch of his hand but also, in reverse, if someone no more than touched his garment. The Gospel relates that a woman who suffered from a flow of blood approached him from behind. 'Jesus said, "Someone touched me; I felt a power going forth from me".' (Lk 8:46). This example demonstrates what bodily touch could bring about. How much more must have taken place when Jesus embraced someone out of his own initiative? In the encounter with Lazarus, it was Jesus who flowed over with *agapē* or love for this disciple. The same word is also used for John, 'the disciple whom Jesus loved'.

Thomas Aquinas (1223–74), the great Christian thinker, asked himself: what kind of love was this that moved back and forth between these two – and why did Jesus love him?

> But he loved John above the others with a special love. There were three reasons for this. First, because of his penetrating understanding: for teachers especially love their intelligent students ... Secondly, because of his purity, for he was a virgin ... Thirdly, because of his youth, for we have tender feelings for the young and weak.[1]

For Thomas there are three reasons for Jesus' great love for John: John was an exceptional thinker, someone who had preserved purity or, in a certain sense, virginity in himself, and was of the same age as Jesus.

Under the cross this same *agapē* connected John with Jesus' mother. Here also it is worth picturing the scene as vividly as possible and transporting ourselves, as it were, into the soul experiences of John, Mary and Jesus. What took place when Jesus connected these two individuals with each other under the cross? If it were merely on a human level – we are familiar with something similar in the last phase of a human life – it could be an expression of stepping back: now you have to find your way together. It is cold comfort when a dying person connects those remaining behind with each other. The dying mother who has to leave her child behind entrusts the child to the care of an adult. She has no other choice. This is not what happened here, for Jesus said something quite exceptional; to his mother he said, 'Woman, see, that is your son', and to John, 'See, that is your mother' (Jn 19:26f). He who is himself the Son gives the sonship to John. We should take these words literally: henceforth you are the son. In other words, in you, John, I live on; henceforth I shall overshadow you in your connection with the mother – an expression of the most profound connection. In all times, the great mystics have sensed and experienced it in this way.

Finally, there is a third expression of *agapē* that indicates that John occupied a special place. Not only did he receive this love from the one who is all love, but toward the end of his life he was able to radiate this love out to others. As presbyter, eldest, he summarised the quintessence of his life in the famous words, 'Children, love one another'.[2] Here also, John used the word that expresses the highest form of love, *agapē,* the unconditional love that asks nothing in return, it only gives.

Let us pause and try to form a concrete picture of what *agapē* is. First of all, the word is used for the love that emanates from God the Father toward his creation: 'The Father showed his love for the world through this, that he offered up his only Son. From now on, no one shall perish who fills himself with his power; indeed he shall win a share of the life that is beyond time' (Jn 3:16). This is an expression of *agapē* to give and to ask nothing in return. It is an unconditional handing over. How can we picture this?

John said God is love. John was completely taken into this love by Jesus' call. This connection culminated at the Last Supper. John lay at the breast of Jesus – close to his heart. Rudolf Steiner once said, 'It expresses the relationship of the pupil to the initiate. "He whom the Lord loved" is the most intimate, the most deeply initiated pupil'.[3] In this context the word 'pupil' of course does not mean that he was something like an apprentice under a master. To be a pupil means literally and figuratively to be touched by an initiate. The touch is a spiritual transfer, a transfer of the power of *agapē* to the pupil.

We could express the extraordinary nature of John in contrast to that of Paul even more succinctly in a single sentence. Paul overcame his own ego and said, 'Not I, but Christ lives in me' (Gal 2:22). John could supplement this sentence with 'and I live in Christ'. Even though this appears like an ideal for the distant future, every human being may experience a first, perhaps indefinite, awareness of this: Christ lives in me – and I live in him. Something of that becomes a reality when a communion at the altar becomes a real 'communion', a communicating, an exchange. Many people think that they only receive something in the communion. But when the priest in the Act of Consecration of Man (the sacrament in the Christian Community) receives the communion, he speaks of an exchange in the words, 'Take me as you have given yourself to me'.

That is an expression of Johannine Christianity, when a human being experiences not only 'He is in me' but 'I give the best in me to him: take me'. In the moment the communion becomes a giving and taking, we ourselves become like John. In this sense, the early church father Origen spoke about human beings as followers of John:

> It can be said that the gospels are the first fruits of Holy Scripture. But the first of the gospels is the Gospel of St John, the significance of which cannot be grasped by anyone who has not himself lain at the breast of Jesus, and has from him received Mary, so that she has also become his mother. Thus he must … become a second John and, like John, become a Jesus under Jesus as it were.[4]

This indeed is the meaning of the words, 'Woman, see, that is your Son'. Origen understood this to signify that with these words John had received the sonship, that John incorporated the Son, one could say, and had become the son of Mary. Origen then extended

6. JOHN: THE IMITATION OF CHRIST

John the Baptist and John the Evangelist, by Zanobi Machiavelli, c. 1470, National Gallery, London.

this to every human being who reads John's Gospel, and said: You must become John. To gain access to this gospel you have to lie at the breast of Jesus yourself, you have to entrust yourself fully to him. Only those can comprehend John's Gospel who have become a second John themselves. In this way Origen sets humanity the task to become John.

This does not signify the end of the profound connection between John and Jesus that is expressed in such monumental words in the story of the Last Supper. We can search for traces of John in subsequent lives with the question of how Johannine Christianity developed further in him. An old spiritual tradition says the greatest initiate of the West, Christian Rosenkreutz, was the same individuality as John. The fruit of this connection with Jesus lived on in him. For as John rested at the breast of Jesus during the Last Supper, of this high initiate it was said that he was a 'grain buried in the breast of Jesus'.[5] It is difficult to imagine a more profound connection of a human being with Jesus than one that had penetrated into the heart, into the deepest core.

In the Gospel of John we can already find expressions of this indwelling; John the Evangelist is able to penetrate into the being, the core, the heart of Jesus. The early Christian authors experienced that the seven 'I AM' sayings represent Christ's indwelling in John. Origen wrote:

> He who lay at the breast of Jesus, to him God entrusts the greatest and most perfect words about Jesus. None of the other evangelists revealed His divinity as purely as John who presents Him to us as he says, 'I am the light of the world; I am the way, the truth and the life; I am the resurrection; I am the door; I am the good shepherd — and in the Apocalypse: I am the alpha and the omega, the beginning and the goal, the first and the last.'[6]

It is this human being who made his 'I' into an organ with which to receive and carry the 'I' of Jesus, not in the sense of an *imitatio Christi,* an imitation of Christ, in which one follows him from a distance and will meet him in the far distant future, but as an immediate presence, as indwelling of Jesus.

According to Origen, John was not only the first among the four

6. JOHN: THE IMITATION OF CHRIST

evangelists but he was also the first among human beings. The 'I AM' sayings – which occur only in the Gospel of John – are expressions of the human being who has achieved the strongest, most intimate, most profound connection with Jesus.

A forgotten chapter in Christianity

How did this connection come into being? In the limited space of one chapter, I have to refer here to the result of several theological research studies: John is the same as Lazarus who was raised from the dead. This identification has not only been described in many places in anthroposophical literature but it is also mentioned in regular theology here and there.

The turning point in his destiny is at the moment when Lazarus is raised from the dead, and when this rich young man, in a certain sense, loses everything and receives his new name, John. The name John (*Ioanēs* in Greek) is not a proper name; it is an indication of a spiritual rank. (*Ioanēs* is the Greek form of a Hebrew name meaning *Yahweh is merciful*.) Rudolf Steiner even called it a generic name: 'John is the name for everyone who is raised from the dead.'[7] How was the connection with the divine achieved? Not by human capacities but by the working of God's mercy that penetrated deeply into this human being and raised him from the dead.

We need to consider this more thoroughly. The first thing to notice is that, unlike anywhere else in the Gospel, Jesus is intensely moved, as if 'turned inside out' in his soul. The particular Greek words used here *(enebrimēsato tō pneumati)* indicate profound agitation of the spirit, because in that moment he became conscious of the possibility of the resurrection. In this human being, in this single raising, he must have foreseen the goal, not only his own goal, but the goal of all of humanity, which is destined to participate in the resurrection. He became conscious of his own resurrection potential. It also occurred when he raised the daughter of Jairus and the youth of Nain, but in Lazarus – shortly before his own death on the cross and resurrection – we see him raising a person he loved. The ninth century scholar John Scotus Eriugena said of John the Evangelist, in relation to his unique place in the circle of disciples:

John, therefore, was not a human being but more than a human being when he flew above himself and all things that are. Transported by the ineffable power of wisdom and by purest keenness of mind, he entered into that which is beyond all things.[8]

In Lazarus, who became John, a human being attained perfection and participated in the resurrection. After he was raised, not only did Christ live in him but he also lived in Christ. From that moment, this human being was complete, as each human being can become complete when he goes the way of the imitation of Christ in his own manner. John was the first. After this, Lazarus-John received a new quality, a new nature that was completely his own.

Two particular features characterise Johannine Christianity. The first is its lofty height: no human being, no evangelist was capable of rising as high as John, the Eagle. At a far advanced age, when he was presbyter in Ephesus, he wrote his Gospel from the perspective of the eagle.

The Gospel of John is no eyewitness account, as some people believe. It was written by someone who, after many years of meditation and prayer, was able to describe the life of Jesus as the last fruit of his Christian initiation, from the highest perspective of *agapē*.

In all times, people have experienced this to a certain extent, not only in his choice of words but especially because in the rhythm of his language, the melody of his language – no other gospel was so 'musically' composed as that of John – John was able to put the life of Jesus on the stage, as it were, in a powerful harmony of story lines. No doubt this is one of the reasons why this Gospel is read at the side of people who have died. It is an old custom, particularly in eastern Christianity, to read the Gospel of John for someone who has died; it is a picture of a completed course of life, the perfect panorama.

The highest viewpoint is the prime characteristic of John's gospel. Besides this, Thomas Aquinas noted that this 'eagle' was capable at the same time of descending into the deepest depths. Thomas discovered that in no other gospel are Jesus' emotions described as eloquently as in the Gospel of John. As John manifests more clearly than the other evangelists the divine nature and power of Christ, so he also relates his weaknesses more clearly: the fact that he wept, that he was moved — everything that expressly shows the passion of the human nature in Christ.⁹

This is a forgotten but precious chapter in Christianity, interesting to trace through the gospels. Where did Jesus show his emotions? We too often imagine him as a person who is exalted far above all emotion. When he prayed – this too is a part of reality – he went up a mountain and spoke his prayer as a sovereign individual on behalf of humanity. But there was also the painful impotence, the despair of Gethsemane.

The writer of the Letter to the Hebrews who, in the view of some authors, came from the school of John the Evangelist, said about Jesus:

> In the days of his earthly incarnation he offered up prayers and entreaties to him who had the power to save him out of the might of death. With intense cries of pain and with tears he offered up his soul, and he was heard because of his readiness to fulfil destiny. He conducted himself like that, although he was the Son. Through his suffering he learned obedience. (Heb 5:7f).

In the same chapter in which the writer of this letter also called Jesus the exalted High Priest of the Order of Melchizedek, he evoked this image of Jesus as powerless and imploring God. And it is John who draws our attention to these two exceptional qualities so that, thanks to his Gospel, we can picture Jesus on the one hand as the Son of God who reaches into boundless heights and, on the other hand, as the Son of Man who is deeply connected with human nature and human weakness. John is the evangelist who connects the highest with the lowest. That is Johannine Christianity.

If we read the Gospel of John from this point of view, from the beginning to the end we will recognise the expressions of this form of Christianity, which connects the heights with the depths, spirit and matter, light and darkness. 'And the light shines in the darkness; and the darkness has not accepted it' (Jn 1:5). The light connects with the darkness – that is characteristic for John's style. He did not write, *'but the darkness has not accepted it'*; he wrote the word *and*. 'The light shines in the darkness *and* the darkness has not accepted it.' There is no judgment.

He is the evangelist who penetrates into matter. 'And the Word became flesh' (Jn 1:14). John was the only evangelist to show that this union of Jesus with the physical world became offensive (*skandalon*, Jn 6:61). When Jesus spoke of eating and drinking 'the earthly body of the Son of Man and ... his blood,' even the disciples could not bear it: 'These are hard and difficult words; who can bear to hear them?' (Jn 6:53, 60). Jesus recognised the offensiveness of these words but irrevocably must fulfil the way from the heights of the spirit to the depths of matter to the end. The view that matter can be penetrated by spirit is part of Johannine Christianity. Expressed in different words, for John, Christ did not only come to redeem humanity: he came to redeem humanity *and* the earth.

Earth, water and blood

At this point, I want to throw more light on the theme of 'earth' in order to illustrate the connection with the earth, in addition to the spiritual character of the Gospel of John. John is the only evangelist who described a composition of seven signs in the life of Christ. The Greek word John used here, *semeion,* indicates that it is an earthly, visible sign that at the same time points to a higher reality. It incorporates both the world of spirit and the world of matter. Thus John described seven signs which, like runes or a script, ask the human being to read and understand them. But the signs place us before riddles. To most Christians today the marriage at Cana in Galilee has no meaning whatever. How is it possible to change water into wine? Humanly speaking we cannot picture that.

Perhaps we could still view the marriage at Cana symbolically but in the subsequent signs the physical component becomes very obvious, even a *skandalon* as mentioned above. 'If you do not eat the earthly body of the Son of Man and drink his blood, you have no life in you' (Jn 6:53). This is the characteristic of Johannine descriptions: the light penetrates into the darkness; Christianity becomes flesh and blood, it becomes earthly reality.

We can trace this motif of the embodiment literally through all

Johannine documents. John has a unique connection with the blood of the Crucified One. This blood 'speaks', one could say. We know the expression of 'speaking blood' from the beginning of the Bible, where something extraordinary is said of the blood of Abel, who had been killed. Yahweh spoke to Cain, 'The voice of your brother's blood is crying to me from the ground' (Gen 4:10). It is an impressive picture: God knows us through and through. He hears the blood. Thus the blood of Jesus 'speaks' when he dies on the cross. For this reason this disciple, who experienced Jesus' love, documented with the greatest precision and care, that blood and water flowed from the wounds of the Crucified One. 'He who saw it has testified to it, and his testimony is true. And he knows that he is speaking the truth, so that you also may find the way of faith' (Jn 19:35). Nowhere is John as emphatic as here, when he testifies of the blood that flowed into the earth.

Finally, the motif of blood and water that 'speak' occurs in the first Letter of John in the enigmatic words:

> He it is who comes close to us in the elements water and blood: Jesus Christ. He does not come close to us in water only, but in water and in blood. And in the element air, the Spirit makes us aware of his nearness, for the Spirit is the truth. Thus we have a threefold witness to his presence: through the Spirit, through the water and through the blood; and these three are one. (1 Jn 5:6–8).

The evangelist made an enigmatic indication here that points to the mystery of the transubstantiation. Water, blood and the spirit are the witnesses. In the Eucharist the mystery is enacted anew when, at the altar, wine and water come together in the chalice, and the spirit, the sacramental word, is spoken over the two substances. In the Christian ritual these Johannine words becomes reality. The mystery of the transubstantiation is enacted between water, wine and word.

The alchemists, who enacted a special form of Christianity in which spirit and matter penetrate each other, made John their patron saint. They called him John the Alchemist. As expressed by them, the goal of the alchemists was to penetrate into the interior of the earth.

They said: Visit the interior of the earth, bring it to perfection, and you will find the hidden stone, the Philosophers' Stone. This Stone can be found only if a human being penetrates into the secret of matter. The first to achieve this was John the Evangelist.

Additional descriptions from legends and mysticism

There is a legend that relates that, from his 27th to his 33rd year, John was an eyewitness of the life of Jesus. Lazarus was raised five weeks before Golgotha. John's path was described by the mystic, Anne Catherine Emmerich, as follows. From his 27th year, John followed Jesus and then also the disciples. His wealth enabled him to support Jesus and the entire circle of disciples financially. He also used his wealth to support the beginnings of Christianity. He was a person in high standing until the moment when he went through initiation, his raising from the dead. He was then no longer trusted, and both the Pharisees and the Romans wanted him killed.

The legends tells that, after Golgotha, John stayed in the Holy Land for another thirteen years. He lived in Nazareth, close to Mary, remote from the persecutions of the Christians, and could covertly support the beginnings of Christianity, both financially and spiritually. He remained in Nazareth and took care of Mary, while the other disciples spread Christianity.

In those early days the first Christians recounted all the events from Jesus' life again and again. Some of the church fathers reported that when one of the disciples spoke of Jesus their face would take on an expression similar to that of Jesus. Whenever a disciple spoke, the resurrection was a recognisable reality. The testimony was no pale memory but visible, audible, tangible reality.

When the persecutions of the Christians intensified after AD 46 John fled with Mary to Ephesus. (Anne Catherine Emmerich indicated in her visions where they had lived, and in 1891 two monks found the foundation of a house there that was dated to the first century.) After Mary's death in the year 56 John continued to live in Ephesus for another 44 years, and the other apostles frequently visited him. During those years the gospels were written. John was one of the last to write his Gospel. Together with Paul he founded a Christian community in

Ephesus. He also made a journey with his sisters Mary and Martha to the valley of the Rhône in France, where there is an interesting legend around the town of Saintes-Maries-de-la-Mer. According to the story, Mary Magdalene landed there and travelled far into the interior with her sister Martha. John accompanied his sisters to the Rhône Valley and then returned to Ephesus.

In the year 70, the Jews revolted against the Romans who then destroyed the temple. The persecutions of the Christians intensified again after the year 95 under Emperor Domitian and became so bad that John went to the Holy Land again to help Christians flee to other countries. In the end he was himself arrested and taken to Rome

John the Evangelist with Prochoros. Seventeenth century icon. Byzantine Museum, Athens.

where his head was shaved and he was immersed in a barrel filled with hot oil. After having survived this torture he spent the rest of his life in exile. He spent part of this time on the island of Patmos where, at age 95, he dictated the Apocalypse to his scribe Prochoros.

When in 96 Domitian was assassinated, John was able to return to Ephesus and had a period of relative calm. There he wrote the three Letters of John, and at age 98 he finally dictated the Gospel of John to Prochoros. The story says that when he dictated the prologue, Prochoros fell down as if dead. The power of these mantric words was so great that someone who heard them for the first time could not remain standing.

On June 24 of the year 100, John the Evangelist died on the day of the birth of his namesake, John the Baptist.

From the Gospel and legends, together with what the mystics related, we can form a fuller picture of the remarkable figure of John.

PART III
Early Christian Movements

7
Esoteric Petrine Christianity
John van Schaik

Rejoice, brother body, and forgive me, because from now on, here I am ready to satisfy your desires willingly, ready to come to your help in need!

Thomas of Celano, The Life of St Francis of Assisi, (2 Cel 211)

Encratism

Encratism was an important phenomenon in early Syrian Christianity and also in the Egyptian desert. Encratites were a group of Jewish Christians who followed Christ by practising extremely strict asceticism. (The word 'Encratite' is derived from the Greek *enkrateia,* meaning self-control). In the eyes of the Orthodox (eastern) church Encratites were viewed as heretics. Tatian, who wrote the *Diatesseron* (harmonisation of the gospels), was an Encratite. Irenaeus of Lyon (*c.* AD 180) even called the Encratites Tatiani, followers of Tatian.

The aim of the Encratites was to return to the original unity with God before the fall into sin. They considered sexual intercourse (of Adam and Eve) to be the cause of the fall. Ever since, human beings have had corrupted bodies in which the devil has free play. Therefore, all bodily desire had to be banished, so that they no longer lived as the 'second Adam' after the fall, but as the 'first Adam' from before the fall. Then the separation would be overcome and the two Adams would become one again. By leading a virginal life the human being was to become an angel, a Son of God, a resurrected one.

This was based on the Bible, including Mark 12:25 where Jesus says, 'When the resurrection of the dead comes, human beings will neither marry nor be given in marriage, for then they are of similar nature to the angels in the spiritual worlds'. According to the

Encratites, Jesus was the perfect ascetic, for he experienced suffering to the ultimate extreme. Besides the consistent struggle against the desires of the body, continuous prayer was the means to 'go into your innermost room' (Mt 6:6) so as to 'establish the Kingdom of God' in the soul.

The way through the body

What actually happens during such strict asceticism? To discover this we need to consult Rudolf Steiner. The Encratites sought God by means of abstinence. The body and all physical forces were subjected to the spirit. To achieve this the body had to be chastised. The resulting pain results in an awareness of the physical forces working in the body. Under normal circumstances we hardly have any awareness of our body, but as soon as we have a headache we become conscious of it. Under normal circumstances we are only conscious of our passions, emotions and desires: in other words our astral body. And when we are healthy we are hardly conscious of that health; we hardly have any consciousness of our vitality or etheric body, except when we are tired, for then we suddenly experience our etheric body. The ascetics tried to get past the astral body, as it were, and past the etheric body to the physical body.

We experience our astral body only when we step outside it and observe it with our 'I': *I* feel joy or sadness, *I* feel like eating something. The 'I' then faces the joy, the sadness or the desire of the astral body. The 'I', or consciousness, thus has to separate itself from the astral body. And similarly with the etheric body. We only become conscious of it when we step out of it and face it, and when the 'I' and the astral body have freed themselves from the etheric body (and physical body).

And in a further stage, we develop consciousness of the forces in the physical body when we become able to observe that body from outside, when the 'I', the astral body and the etheric body have all freed themselves from the physical body. According to Steiner, these several separations take place when we are ill but also on a certain mystical path of initiation. We may call it 'the path of initiation into the body'.

7. ESOTERIC PETRINE CHRISTIANITY

This was the way of the Encratites. They consciously loosened the physical body from the etheric body, the astral body and the 'I'. They followed the ascetic path completely consciously. First they loosened the astral body from the 'I' by controlling desire and emotion. Then the etheric body was loosened from the physical body by strict asceticism. The result of this was that the body began to die. A near-death experience occurred. In this way the ascetics experienced the divine forces in the body; these are the creative forces that worked at the beginning of human development to build up the body. In terms of the Trinity, one could say they are the Father forces. The ascetic brought these forces to consciousness.[1]

When Jesus asked the apostles who they thought he was, Peter gave the answer that he was the Son of the living God (see Chapter 1). According to Steiner, Peter could give this answer only out of 'divine-spiritual forces far below the threshold of consciousness [that] spoke in these words. Indeed, these are the most profound forces in the human being.'[2] These divine-spiritual powers were brought to consciousness in asceticism. The primal Father Ground was brought to consciousness, which restored the original unity in Paradise. In this way, the ascetics individualised and brought to consciousness the Father, who could be experienced in the physical heredity of the Jewish people. That is the esoteric path of Petrine Christianity. In the following, we will describe a number of ascetic mystics who went on this path to the Father God through the body.

Simeon the Stylite

There are many biographies of Encratites in which we can trace how they worked. One of the better known ones was the famous Syrian ascetic Simeon the Stylite. His biographer was Theodoret, Bishop of Cyrrhus (393 – *c.* 460). Theodoret played an important part in the Synod of Ephesus in 431. In his work *Religious History (Philostheos historia)* he described no less than 70 Syrian ascetics and monks of his time. The work dates from 443 or 444. Theodoret himself knew a number of these ascetics, and Simeon was undoubtedly among them.

Simeon the Stylite (*stylus* means column) was born into a family of Christian farmers in northwestern Syria in 390. He entered a

PART III: EARLY CHRISTIAN MOVEMENTS

The funeral of St Ephrem of Syria; in the centre is Simeon the Stylite on his pillar. Emanuele Zanfurnari (c.1500), Pinacoteca Vaticana.

monastery near Antioch at a young age, but because of his fanatical asceticism he was expelled after ten years. He then chose an Encratite lifestyle and withdrew for the rest of his life into the desert, where he died at age 70. Simeon is known mostly because he withdrew into the desert on a pillar that was initially about two metres (6 ft) high, but at the end of his life it was about 18 metres (60 ft). There he stood, with his feet chained to the pillar. Of course, he dedicated himself to constant prayer. But he was not lonely; he became so famous that people came to his pillar from all over the world to admire him, to ask advice or to be healed. He was able to convert entire tribes called Ishmaelites in his biography.

As a child, Simeon was in church where he implored 'the one who wants to save all human beings' to show him the 'perfect way to piety'.[3] He had a vision in which he was told to dig a deep pit. Whenever in the vision he wanted to take a rest he was told to keep on digging until the pit was deep enough for a 'secure building'. The vision is not explained, but we may conjecture that the pit is a picture of the body into which he had to descend so as to build it up anew. Digging a pit may also indicate digging a tomb in which one dies in order to rise again in Christ.

Simeon became a monk, but his asceticism was much more rigorous than that of the other monks, who ate only every other day, while Simeon did not eat for a whole week. One day Simeon surprised another monk because blood was trickling down from under his habit. It turned out that for weeks already Simeon had tied a very rough rope tightly around his waist. For that reason he eventually had to leave the monastery in order to prevent him from doing damage to those with weaker physical conditions.[4]

Simeon then departed for the desert where he regularly observed forty day periods of fasting, as Moses and Elijah also did, and as Jesus did in his forty days in the desert. He spent the first days of these fasts standing and singing hymns; then he sat down, and toward the end of the forty days he lay 'half dead' on the ground. But many years later he was able to remain standing for the full forty days, 'when he had received grace from on high'. Unceasingly, 'he kept his eye on God and forced himself to contemplate the highest heavens'. His fame spread, and from all over the world adventurers came to him, including Ishmaelites – the biography mentions tens of thousands – and Himyarites from the southwest Arabian peninsula.

One day, an Ishmaelite promised to eat no more meat but he broke his promise by eating a bird. As he was eating, the bird changed into a stone. The poor Ishmaelite hurried to Simeon who forgave him. The story reminds us of the apocryphal *Arabic Gospel of the Infancy* and of the Koran (5:110), in which Jesus brings clay birds to life. Simeon also enabled the barren queen of the Ishmaelites to bear a child. He was in constant contact with God. After his death, his body did not decompose.

'Grace bestowed on him from on high' enabled Simeon to bear his physical torments and perform his miracles. That was similarly the case with St Anthony, the desert anchorite in the Egyptian desert, in the fourth century. While Simeon, in his vision, dug his own grave, Anthony literally lay down in his tomb for long periods of time, without food. When his friends opened the tomb, he lay there as if dead. In the tomb he was called back to life by God. A divine light-beam penetrated the darkness of the tomb, all the demons fled and God said that he would henceforth always be Anthony's helper. His biography relates:

> When he heard that, he rose and prayed. And he received so much strength that he perceived that his body had more strength than before.[5]

When he then reappeared from his isolation it was as if he came out of a sanctuary 'where he had been initiated in the mysteries and inspired by God'.

Anthony and Simeon went through an initiation, down into the body, and rose up in their glorified bodies. They built up their bodies anew. Anthony literally rose from his grave, which is a metaphor for the body. The body was restored to its original state before the fall.

Alexius

The Christian ascetic path was very popular in the Syrian and Egyptian deserts. But this form of asceticism also developed in the west. The 'Life of Simeon' relates that figurines of Simeon could be bought in every shop in Rome. At the beginning of the fifth century Alexius, the son of a wealthy couple of the ruling class, lived in Rome. During his wedding night, he decided not to consummate the marriage but to put himself in service of God. He fled in the night and went to Edessa in Syria. There he dedicated himself for seventeen years to the 'service of the Lord'. He tortured his body in service of God. He was 'worthy of entering Paradise,' and 'stands close to God and the heavenly kingdom'.

This made him famous in the region around Edessa. Many people visited him, which distracted him from his ascetic practices. He fled and took a ship bound for Tarsus but due to a storm he ended up in Rome again. He returned to his parents, who, without recognising him, took him into their home where he lived under the stairs for another seventeen years, mocked by the servants who fed him scraps and leftovers. When he heard the lamentations of his parents and his wife who were missing him, 'they did not touch him; he was too strongly focused on God'. When he died he went straight to Paradise. 'He could see God himself'. After his death, his parents found a letter on his emaciated body in which he had written who he was.

The story of Alexius' life was popularised in the eleventh century by the French *Vie* or *Chanson de saint Alexis.* This inspired others like Pope Leo IX (1002–54) and Peter Damian (the reforming Benedictine monk, *c.* 1007–72) to write of Alexius' life in Latin verse. Versions of the song circulated in some western monasteries. Alexius was viewed as having led a pure apostolic way of life. That was the way to serve God, not the way in which fat, rich priests lived. It is also the moral message of the Life of Alexius. For a week before his death, there was great consternation among the inhabitants of Rome when they heard a heavenly voice announcing that Rome would collapse if the body of the Man of God was not found. Everyone started looking for the good man. When they finally found him, many wealthy Romans felt urged by Alexius to share their wealth with the poor. Apparently, God wanted to indicate through Alexius that Rome should strive for inner wealth and sobriety.

Francis of Assisi

In the eleventh century the Life of Alexius became extremely popular. Asceticism was an important motif in the Gregorian church reformation. Hermits and anchorites were everywhere, and often seen as heretics in the eyes of church. Thus an extensive tradition of asceticism with strong mystical traits arose also in the west. Sometimes it led to the same kinds of ascetic excesses as in the east. Not everyone supported that. For instance, Eckbert, the brother of the ascetic mystic Elisabeth of Schönau (1129–64), related:

> She was able to leave the body in spirit and behold visions of God's mystery ... Often and regularly, a certain kind of suffering assailed her on Sundays and feast days, and she was seized by great fear, until she fell down as if her soul had left her, so that there was no semblance of life or movement to be observed. When she then, after a long ecstasy, slowly came to herself again she would suddenly break out in the most divine words in Latin, a language she had never learned.[6]

But Elisabeth's spiritual friend Hildegard of Bingen (1098–1179) was very critical of Elisabeth's asceticism. She wrote to her in a letter that moderation is of greater worth. According to Hildegard, such strict asceticism made one susceptible to the devil.

The best known ascetic mystic in the west is St Francis of Assisi (1181–1226). His story is well-known. He was born into a well-to-do family in Assisi. In his younger years, he led a loose life. When he was 26 he was called by God. In the valley of Spoleto he had a heavenly vision. A voice asked him, 'Who is more, a servant or a lord?' The voice told him to return to Assisi. This experience turned Francis 'from a Saul into a Paul' (2 Cel 6).[7] Francis was converted. He made a pilgrimage to Rome, where he joined the beggars on the steps of St Peter's. When at home again, he resided amid lepers. Then followed the famous event in the little church of San Damiano that was about to collapse. He entered and saw that the lips of the Christ figure on the cross were moving. Christ spoke the famous words, 'Francis, go and repair my house which, as you can easily see, is in ruins' (2 Cel 10). Right away

7. ESOTERIC PETRINE CHRISTIANITY

Giotto, Francis receiving the stigmata. Basilica de S. Francesco, Assisi

he began to restore the church, and when that was accomplished after two years, he looked around for another little church. But his task was not to restore physical churches, rather it should be understood in a spiritual sense. When Francis requested an audience with the Pope, he remembered that he had had a vision a few days before:

> In a dream he [the Pope] had seen the Basilica of St John Lateran [in Rome] that threatened to fall into ruin, and a small, religious, but despicable-looking man was holding it up on his shoulders to keep it from falling. 'Certainly,' he thought, 'he is the one who will sustain the church of Christ through his works and his words.' (2 Cel 17).

This vision shows that Petrine Christianity has two sides: an exoteric Petrine Christianity and an esoteric Petrine Christianity. The visible church of St Peter is built on the apostle Peter as the rock. At first, Francis thought that he had to restore that church, but that was not the case. He had to rebuild the church in a mystical sense.

Love for the Creator

Francis was famous for his love for the creation and the Creator. And although he would have much preferred to immediately leave this earth, he took great joy in the creation. The world is both a battleground and the bright mirror of God's goodness (2 Cel 165). In every creature he recognised the Father-Creator:

> He rejoiced in all the works of the Lord's hands and through those joyful visions he perceived the life-giving reason and the cause (2 Cel 165).

Francis beheld the creative forces that work in the creation. He beheld the Creator Father, not in heaven but in his creation. He beheld the Father Spirit in the heights working creatively in the depths. And because he was a friend of the Creator, other creatures honoured him: he called all living beings his brothers. He called his own body Brother Ass. When he was seriously ill, he addressed his body as follows:

> Rejoice, brother body, and forgive me, because from now on, here I am ready to satisfy your desires willingly, ready to help in your need (2 Cel 211).

Francis had complete consciousness over the state of his physical body. He experienced the creative forces of his body. He was able to bear the pain and suffering this entailed because Christ lived in his soul. He died, as it were, in Christ and rose in Christ. As a sign of this, two years before his death he received the stigmata. These are rarely bestowed on human beings, and Francis was one of the first. The Spanish mystic Teresa of Avila (1515–82) and Therese Neumann (1898–1962) from Bavaria as well as the anthroposophist Judith von Halle also received them.

The stigmata gave Francis the ability to exercise power himself over the creation. When his eye disease had to be treated with a burning hot iron, Francis spoke to the fire:

> Brother fire, marvellous among all the other creatures, the Most High has made you strong and beautiful and useful. Be benevolent to me now and be kind to me, for I have loved you in the Lord. I beseech the wonderful God who created you to temper your heat a bit so that you will burn gently and I will be able to withstand you. (2 Cel 166).

And indeed, the fire did not harm him. The physician was struck dumb and exclaimed that it was a miracle. And Francis' biographer, Thomas de Celano wrote, 'I believe that Francis has returned to original innocence' (3 Cel 14). 'Original innocence' – that is the original state of Adam in Paradise.

Miracles

Since Francis knew the creative forces in nature, he was also able to use these forces to perform miracles, both during his life and thereafter. The most beautiful description of a miracle performed by Francis is that of the old recluse Praxedes who had lived for forty years in her cell. One day she broke her leg, so her cell had to be broken open to help her, but she did not want that. She called Francis to help her. Then she went into ecstasy:

> And then the most benevolent Father, dressed in the white robes of glory descended into that dark prison and began to speak in a sweet tone, saying, 'Get up, blessed daughter, get up and fear not. Receive the gift of perfect health and keep your vow unbroken.' Then taking her by the hand, he got up and disappeared. She then started to turn to and fro in her cell and could not understand what the Servant of God had done to her, for she thought she was still dreaming. At last, she went to the window and made her usual summoning gesture. A monk quickly ran over to her and, astonished beyond all belief, he said to her, 'What happened to you, O mother, that you were able to get up?' Thinking that she was still dreaming and not recognising him, she asked to have the fire lit. As soon as the light was brought to her, she returned to her senses and, no longer feeling any pain, she recounted the entire occurrence. (3 Cel 181).

It was as if Christ himself descended into her cell in the guise of Francis and healed her.

Conclusion

Hildegard of Bingen had it right; history confirms this. In the eyes of the church – east and west – strict asceticism was often viewed as an excess, and rejected as heretical. The emphasis in mysticism moved more and more to asceticism of the soul: the practice of virtue. That is more in the nature of Paul. Mysticism became soul mysticism. The ascetic mysticism of Petrine Christianity, the initiation in the body, was no longer fashionable in the Renaissance.

8
Dionysius the Areopagite, the First Christian Mystic
Christine Gruwez

The Word that was spoken by the Father and could become human being remains unspeakable, and that which I have comprehended and known remains unknown.

Dionysius the Areopagite

Paul and Dionysius the Areopagite

About thirty years after the crucial event of Christianity, the crucifixion and resurrection of Jesus Christ, the apostle Paul stood on the Areopagus to speak to the wise men of the Athenian Council. Paul had been in the city for a few days. Athens was the centre of culture and learning at the time. Most of the population of course were not Jewish, but pagan.

As an itinerant preacher and proclaimer of a new kind of teaching, Paul had drawn the attention of the Epicureans and the Stoics. His words must have caused such astonishment that he was invited to the Areopagus. This event, described in Chapter 17 of the Acts, is from many points of view a historic moment. Paul, who had been led into the third heaven and touched by the risen Christ, allowing the new Adam to be born in him, stood facing this select group of men and one woman who represented the height of wisdom and culture at the time. It was the moment when Greek thinking, which developed out of the mystery schools, encountered a living witness of the Mystery of Golgotha. The ancient mysteries led up to this pivotal moment: the wisdom of the old mysteries could now be renewed in the open mystery of the incarnation of God, his death and resurrection.

Paul stood before them as one born into a new-found freedom. This resounded in the confident tone with which he addressed them. With a touch of irony he pointed to the many altars dedicated to a great variety of divinities which he had noticed on his walks through the city, 'Athenians, I see that you are devoted to the gods in every respect. I have gone through your town and have looked at your shrines'. But that was not really the point. What he really wanted to say followed:

> and I have found an altar with the inscription: To THE UNKNOWN GOD. The one whom you revere, without knowing him, he it is whom I proclaim to you.

And then he began to describe this unknown god whose altar he had found in Athens. One of the elements Paul bought is that the unknown god was not to be found in statues and temples made by human hands. After bringing in other elements, he said, 'in him we live and weave and have our being'.

The temple of this unknown god whom Paul proclaimed was to be found in the human being. This is the core of Christianity as it became experience in Paul and which he tirelessly proclaimed.

Paul was treated with disdain and ridiculed. A few listeners said that it was a strange story but that they were willing to hear more about it some other time – a display of wisdom that has hardened into arrogance. We must not forget that Paul at that time was standing in the cultural centre of the Greco-Roman world, where people set the tone and defined culture. They were fully conscious of their position what they represented. Yet few received the message. Two are named in Acts 17:34: Dionysius the Areopagite and the Damaris, who was perhaps the leading priestess in the mystery of Eleusis, the only woman allowed in the Council.

There was a decisive turn in the development of Christianity when Paul crossed the Hellespont from Troy to Neapolis, from Asia Minor into Europe, though the latter was not yet a territorial concept. What happened was that an angel who appeared to Paul as a Macedonian in a nocturnal vision, and called on him to cross the strait to Macedonia

(Acts 16:9). We should be clear that Paul remained in the same cultural world, the world he was familiar with in Asia Minor where he had made his first journey as a preacher. Perhaps this is an even stronger indication of the historic significance of Paul's moment on the Areopagus in Athens.

The speech on the Areopagus had also been prepared in another way when Paul sojourned in Thessalonica, a city that had been founded by a half-brother of Alexander the Great and was at one time the capital of Macedonia. There is a spot in Thessalonica on the top of a hill where, when one looks in the right direction and the weather is favourable, one can see Mount Olympus in the distance, the mythical mountain where the twelve Olympian gods of the Greeks resided. It is not hard to imagine how Paul, in sight of Olympus and the world of the Greek gods, made his first speech to the inhabitants of Thessalonica; and then, with that same image in his mind, he addressed the Council of wise men in Athens. He stood facing the finest flower of Greco-Roman culture without evading confrontation. There these few people were open to Paul's proclamation. This moment is inseparably linked with the figure of Dionysius the Areopagite, no matter how difficult it will be to demonstrate this connection in its actual reality.

Dionysius the Areopagite and his writings

As has been mentioned before, it is interesting that there are no known letters from Paul to a community in Athens. Of other places in Greece where a congregation formed, one or more letters have survived – and there may have been others that have been lost. But why did he not write to an infant congregation in Athens? Was there perhaps no congregation? Or was something born in Athens that developed differently from that which grew in other places that Paul visited?

There is no historical proof of this, but at a certain time in the development of early Christianity some documents came to light that are attributed to the same Dionysius who had heard Paul's speech. These documents are clearly so closely connected with each other that they form a body; one document moves in a natural way to the next

PART III: EARLY CHRISTIAN MOVEMENTS

with the questions arising in one being developed in the next.

There are four tracts of very unequal lengths that form part of this body or *corpus*. There are the two documents that are best known in western Christianity. The first is about the heavenly hierarchies of angels, that gives us a picture of the angelic ranks and their activity. Connected with this, the second document treats of the hierarchy of the church. The two other documents shed light of the connection between Paul and Dionysius, particularly the more extensive one about the divine names.

These four tracts form the principal part of the works of Dionysius the Areopagite and are followed by ten letters whose authenticity, however, is uncertain. These documents first appeared around 530. They were quoted by Severus, a bishop in Antioch, who was suspected of heresy. His adherents used Dionysius' writings to bolster their arguments.

The background to this dispute lies in the first centuries of Christianity when discussions focused on the nature of Jesus Christ, on the relationship between the divine and human nature in Jesus Christ, and how to comprehend this. This led then to doctrines being developed which could be or had to be believed. Almost every century between the fourth and the ninth produced another point of contention related to this question. Councils took place and deliberations among scholars and church fathers, who developed doctrines to settle these conflicts.

Bishop Severus of Antioch was suspected of being a Monophysite. He invoked Dionysius to demonstrate that he was not. A monophysite believes that Christ possessed one single nature, in this case the divine nature. There are several interpretations regarding his human nature, but the human nature is not his real nature, it is only a semblance. The true nature of Jesus Christ is the divine one, and that is the only one; hence *monos* (sole), *physis* (nature): the doctrine of one sole nature.

Then we hear nothing of Dionysius' writings for a while. It is worth noting that these writings were not declared heretical. Quite the contrary: about a hundred years later one of the great Greek church fathers, Maximus the Confessor, an established authority, presented an astonishingly fiery defence of these writings. He said that they touched him to the roots of his soul, and that after reading them and meditating on them he viewed Christianity with different eyes, and was thoroughly changed as a Christian and as a human being. His was but one voice among a many that expressed the same experience, for these writings possess a remarkable power. Their content is not easily accessible if read simply as a theological text: that is not what they are. But if one enters into these writings searching for the deeper layers of meaning of words, then – said Maximus – a world opens that does not cease to nourish us as Christians.

But even greater than the influence they have had in the great tradition of the Greek church, is the importance these writings developed in Latin Christianity.

> Apart from the Bible and the works of Boethius, there is no single work that received such incomparable, overwhelming attention in the west, whether in translation, commentary, quotations, or by forming a kind of encyclopaedic overview, so that one can truly speak of scholarship of the works of the Areopagite.[1]

Church fathers in east and west

In order to complete this picture we have to consider the development of Christianity from the beginning of the fourth century. Two main centres arose. On the one hand from Constantinople orthodox Christianity developed – Greek Orthodox or Byzantine Christianity that also continued in the Russian Orthodox church. On the other hand, in the west Roman Christianity developed its own character. The early church fathers wrote either in Greek and belonged to eastern Christianity (like Origen), or in Latin – like Augustine and Tertullian – and were part of the Roman church.

There is also a factor that goes much deeper than the language one uses to express Christianity in human words. There is a fundamental difference between Greek and Latin. The Greek language is a flexible, living language, a language that makes it possible to create new words that remain transparent to living content. Latin, by contrast, forms and fixes everything with the result that life is closed in and everything becomes rigid. The element that is key in the question as to the nature of Jesus Christ is expressed in Latin with the word *substantia*. But substance is something very close to what we now call matter, which has a fixed, crystallised form. Greek uses the word *ousia,* which means something that is in the process of becoming. These two terms evoke totally different ideas.

Dionysius the Areopagite, who wrote in Greek, is one in the series of important figures of the Greek Christian world including Clement of Alexandria, Origen, the Cappadocian church fathers, Maximus the Confessor, John of Damascus and many others. He forms part of a spiritual stream that existed long before his writings, and continued after these writings were discovered.

In the western world, however, his writings came like a thunderbolt from the blue. Unlike in the Greek context, there is not a single document that can be seen as a predecessor, and there may be just one document in the west that directly builds on the work of Dionysius the Areopagite. It is a completely different situation.

It is true that mysticism developed in the West and that there is a fourteenth-century mystical document, *The Cloud of Unknowing,* whose author is unknown, that is a clear manifestation of the effects of the writings of the Areopagite. Also the circle around the Friend of God from the Oberland, in the same century, bears the stamp of a similar mystical experience. But then we have already entered the field of experience; the line between experience and theology becomes blurred.

In the orthodox Christian world, Dionysius is always called *ho Theo-logos.* That does not mean theologian in the sense of a religious scholar or commentator; it means he who has fathomed the *Logos,* the Word of God, to its deepest depth. It reflects the capacity he possessed to penetrate with clarity of consciousness the Word of God to its full depth, there where it becomes obscure for the human intellect. This enabled him to have what could be called an ultimate connection with the *Logos,* God's creative Word or God's Son.

Legend and influence

In France there is a legend that Christianity was brought there by a bishop with the name of Denis (Dionysius). He died a martyr's death and was buried on Montmartre, the hill of martyrs. In the Christian legend, St Denis is identified with Dionysius the Areopagite. North of Paris there is monastery dedicated to St Denis. Around the year 630 the relics of the bishop-martyr were solemnly entombed in its church. It became a centre of spirituality where in the twelfth-century abbot Suger laid the foundation for the Gothic style of architecture.

In the Middle Ages, France was one of the three great kingdoms that emerged after the Charlemagne's empire was split up. To establish good diplomatic relations with this new kingdom, Michael II, the Byzantine Emperor in Constantinople, sent as a gift a copy of the writings of Dionysius the Areopagite.

The document was of course written in Greek, and King Charles the Bald searched in vain in the various abbeys and monasteries in his realm for someone who could translate these precious documents. But then a 'man from across the sea' appeared at his court, who called himself Johannes Eriugena (meaning born in Erin, Ireland). He received the epithet *Scotus* which was used for anyone who came from Scotland or Ireland. Thus he became known as John Scotus Eriugena. He knew enough Greek to translate the documents into Latin. He even added a document of his own, *De Divisione Naturae,* not only as an elaboration of the doctrine of hierarchies but also to enlarge it to a comprehensive cosmology. He assigned a place to the human being as a kind of tenth rank. This idea was later developed in western Christianity in the School of Chartres.

Dionysius' writings increasingly inspired mystical movements in western Christianity. And a little later, during the Renaissance, Greek was studied again in the west, so that previously unknown writings like those of the Platonic schools became accessible.

It was then that some people noticed that these texts could not possibly be written by Paul's disciple who had heard Paul's speech on the Areopagus, because they contain references and sometimes quotations from documents dating from the fourth and fifth centuries. Dionysius the Areopagite was now for the first time viewed in a different light. In the following centuries research continued into these documents discovering references to other authors including, for instance, the Neoplatonic philosopher Proclus (411–485). The question was definitively resolved around 1895 by Hugo Koch and the Jesuit Josef Stiglmayr, two German philologists, who became famous for this research work. Independently of each other they made it absolutely clear that a disciple of Paul could not have been the author of these documents. It was after this that the author is commonly referred to as Pseudo-Dionysius the Areopagite.

Disciple of Paul?

In Orthodox Christianity, the question of a Pseudo-Dionysius never played any role. In the west, Edith Stein, (1891–1942) a German Carmelite nun, was someone who consistently opposed the idea of a Pseudo-Dionysius.[2] Her argument was that if we do not merely look at the contents of these writings, but live into them, we have an immediate experience of authenticity. Therefore, if someone wanted to create the impression that he was Dionysius the Areopagite, he must have had another reason, rather than – as suggested by Koch and Stiglmayr – simply cleverly making use of the name to promote his own writings. Such ideas of plagiarism or forgery are modern notions, and were unrecognised in the ancient world.

We mention this to show that Dionysius and his writings played a rather ambiguous role in the development of Christianity in the first few centuries, and that even today this figure causes controversy. We could well ask whether the question of *pseudo* or *genuine,* is not a red herring to distract our attention from what the intention of these texts actually is.

Before we can say why someone who is the author of such documents would create the impression of having had a connection with the apostle Paul, I think we need to take another look at the kind of Christianity that Paul represented, at Pauline Christianity. Is there really something like Pauline Christianity? Many people are convinced that there is something called Johannine Christianity; and there are also many things that point to a Petrine Christianity. But is there also be a Pauline Christianity?

The first thing we can establish is that Pauline Christianity is totally oriented and dedicated to the Son, the *Logos* principle in Christianity. That is Paul's connection to all that is Christian. Before the gate of Damascus something touched him. It was not the Christianity of the Father, neither was it the Christianity of the Spirit. What touched him was the Christianity of the divine Son. If we follow this idea and try to show some elements that characterise it, we will be confronted with a number of questions and riddles.

When Paul was touched by the Son, he was also touched by the profound realisation that God's Son became a human being. Early Christianity generally accepted that the incarnation started with the baptism in the Jordan, when Christ was born in Jesus of Nazareth – but it did not end there. It was a beginning. From that instant, the incarnation progressively continued until the ultimate moment when the Son died on the Cross.

The seven Words from the Cross spoken by Jesus Christ and reported by the four evangelists can therefore be regarded as expressions of the last steps in the process of incarnation. This incarnation signifies that the divine nature of Christ and the human nature of Jesus of Nazareth permeated each other so fully, without leaving any 'remnant,' that it became possible for the Son to die in the same way that a human being dies. For that reason we can truly speak of a resurrection. The resurrection only became true – and Paul witnessed to this in his own fervent and passionate way – if God's Son died as a human being, which was made possible by the divine Son becoming totally human.

If we pursue this, the realisation dawns that in this death and resurrection an 'essentially new being' rises up. For the one who is resurrected from death is not only Christ, the Son of God, is not only Jesus of Nazareth – it is the one who, after total interpenetration, entered into death and rose out of death, and in so doing brought the seed of a substance that did not exist on earth before. *When Paul was touched by Christ, he was touched by the risen Christ, he was touched by the one who at the beginning of a process that continues to be brought to realisation, the new resurrected being.* Paul's insight that this being was something new shook him to the core. In a single instant, it burned away, as it were, everything Paul was until that event, so that Paul was born as a new person, as in an initiation.

In place of the old Adam the first beginning of the new Adam was born in Paul. Paul was a witness of the indwelling of the risen Christ. Through this experience alone he distinguished himself from the disciples and apostles who were witnesses of the incarnation of God's Son in Jesus of Nazareth. Something new was beginning: the Christianity that developed out of the mystery of the indwelling of the resurrected Christ could be called Pauline Christianity.

I would add to this that Dionysius' writings – no matter who he may have been – proceeded from a stream of human beings who, like Paul, shared in their inner being this new reality of the risen Christ. We may therefore surmise that Dionysius was not an isolated figure. He indeed was the one who bore witness to this and made himself known by his writings, but the crucial point lies in the spiritual nature of the thoughts of those in whose deepest core the seed of the risen Christ had begun to work.

On the way to the mystery

We may well ask: where will this lead? For Paul, it happened in one concentrated instant. This might be a picture of an initiation that was enacted in such a radical manner as to penetrate into the deepest layers of Paul's individuality and to transform these. It also helps us to understand that for Paul the perpetual experience of the indwelling was so overwhelmingly real that he *had to* speak about it, he *had to* proclaim it. Both in his letters and in the Acts we read of incidents when he was stoned, scourged, chased away, but the moment he was able to pull himself together and stand on his feet, he immediately started speaking about his experience again. The inner force was so strong that he could not but proclaim it.

In Dionysius' writings we can sense that they were created to guard the mystery of the indwelling, to learn how this mystery must be contemplated before it can be proclaimed. The various mystical streams, particularly those in the west, that were inspired by these writings, can be seen in this light. With the greatest possible reverence they quietly approach and protect the mystery of the genuine reality of the presence of God.

Later in the development of Christianity, at the time of the Reformation, there were figures who proclaimed what had been closely guarded for a long time. Perhaps this is the reason that there is a kind of silence round Dionysius' writings: they remain hidden in a kind of mystery. But this mystery will open and become generally accessible.

The question will be whether in the proclamation we can still recognise the experience of the indwelling, whether that experience is still sufficiently protected and nurtured, and whether this will still be something that incessantly works into the world out of someone's inner being, urging them to proclaim it far and wide. Or will it become a proclamation without the experience? These questions can make us ask ourselves what the connection really is between what we speak and what we experience. Do we first have to take a step back – or is it perhaps a step forward – to comprehend what lies at the heart of Dionysius' writings: the unspeakable reality of God's being?

When we live into these writings more deeply we can begin to sense why Dionysius apparently claimed an identity that cannot be proven by historical facts. However, it is striking that Dionysius the Areopagite continuously referred to Paul, or mentioned his travelling companions such as Timothy. It is as if he wanted to indicate that he was not one of Paul's travelling companions in an outer sense, but that the connection was through an inner path.

The unknown and the unknowable god

It is perfectly clear that Dionysius builds on the idea of the unknown god; that is what his thoughts and contemplations revolve around. On the one hand there is the fact that God made himself known, he made himself known in such a way that his Son incarnated into a human body, and that through the Mystery of Golgotha each human being could experience the Risen One inwardly. And on the other hand, there is the mystery that the being of God is unreachable to the grasp of human knowing. Several times he expresses certain forms of knowing as a kind of 'seizing' or 'grasping'. For instance he wrote, 'The divine being is the cause of all that is.'

How can that which is caused by God's being, namely our thinking, grasp this being and come to know it in that way? In that sense the unknown god is also the one who cannot be known. On the other hand, in the incarnation, death and resurrection God brought his essential reality to human beings in the most intimate manner, because he makes himself known in the depths of the human soul.

Dionysius now moved between these two poles. Beginning with his treatise on the divine names, he searched for the manner in which we can guard and preserve the bridge between God and humanity, a bridge that does indeed exist, while at the same time we understand that God's life transcends it. It is often said that his theology is not about transcendence. Transcendence means that God is far removed from humanity; he exists, but we can never reach him. But the way in which Dionysius understood God's Word is that he described that God's knowledge far exceeds human comprehension. That is not the same as the idea that God has removed himself from humanity.

One way in which he demonstrated how God, through the Son, nevertheless approaches humanity, is that God's nature is turned to humanity. That is a key concept in his theology: God turns toward humanity. When someone turns to another, then they stand facing each other. Paul expressed this in his First Letter to the Corinthians (13:12):

Now we still see everything in dark outlines, as in a mirror.
Some day we will see everything face to face.

God turns toward humanity, but that does not mean that we are able to bear the sight of the being of God. As an intermediate stage to help human beings, God does not make his life known as such, even though it is turned to humanity, but makes it known through his names.

Dionysius does this by enumerating the many names of God, one after another, in a kind of song of praise, a hymn. It is no dry recitation. He calls up all the names that God places outside himself in order to make himself known. He says the highest of these names is goodness. Then come light, life, being and countless other names (I am only mentioning the ones at the beginning of the list). But in the names through which God addresses humanity we perceive a descending line. Each of these names could be viewed as a step on a flight of stairs or ladder built between God and humanity. Every name is a step closer to humanity. In each name God expresses and reveals himself. We could also say that with a name he opens an aspect of his being, without disclosing his being as such in a complete revelation. Each name is a partial aspect of the being of God. Goodness stands closest to the fullness of God's true being itself. The picture that Dionysius thus creates is that, as we progress down and come closer to humanity, on each of these steps the fullness of God decreases. When we have arrived at the lowest rung of the ladder, it is very close. God has then expressed himself in a great many names, but the last names contain but little of the absolute fullness of his being. This is the core element in the treatise on the divine names.

Silence is greater than speech

In *Mystical Theology* we find how the way continues after this. The flight of stairs that came into existence when God turned to humanity and expressed himself in all these names, creates the potential for human beings to ascend it. However, there are qualifications, and these express the distinct nature of the inner world of Dionysius. If as human beings we do the same thing as God or even continue it – if we say, 'God is good' – in a certain sense we do the same thing as when God expresses his own nature: we take steps away from God. The more we speak about God, the farther removed from him we become.

Can we come close to God? Certainly, but only on condition that we go in the opposite direction of God's approach to humanity. God comes to humanity by expressing himself; human beings come to God by keeping what God has expressed silently in themselves. Keeping silence in ourselves entails bringing into ourselves – impressing upon ourselves – what has been expressed, and making it part of our own being. In order to enable us to take this into our own being, we must first empty ourselves of all that is attached to our own being, for how can the names God has revealed find a place within us if we are still full of all kinds of things that have to do with our own personality? Paul used the word *kenōsis* when describing this emptying ourselves (Phil 2:7).

This emptying is an element of the silence, for we silence everything in ourselves that would add our own patterns, points of view, ideas, awareness and comments. That we are able to do this, Dionysius said, has to do with the fact that God has made himself known in the most radical sense of the word by sending his own Son to humanity. His Son did not descend down these steps to humanity; he came from God directly through the world of the hierarchies.

Here is the great difference with the Neoplatonic schools, which also developed some of these thoughts. The Neoplatonists describe 'the One' emanating and approaching the world God has created and caused. But Dionysius realised out of his inner Christian experience that this is not enough, and that God's making himself known by letting his Son descend to the created world was more than an approach *to* what is, but was an immersion *into* what is. Since in the Pauline sense, the Son of God can work down into and through human beings, human beings are able to find the way back to God, by climbing every step of the stairway and by emptying themselves. This is the great theme of Paul: not I, but Christ in me.

Thus we have, on the one hand, the way of the descent, which in Dionysian theology and in the Orthodox world is called the *kataphatic* way, the way of speaking out, and on the other hand, the *apophatic* way, the way of keeping silence, the negative way or the way of denial. In the latter we do not say, God is good, because then we move away from God. Instead, we say God is above all good. Similarly we do not say, God is light; but God is above light, or God transcends light. What we express as a kind of affirmation is in essence a denial, but a denial in order to raise the affirmation to a higher level. In such a moment of denial we cannot but turn inward. We distance ourselves from knowing that God is light and good. It is a moment of emptying ourselves, which also means that we rise above ourselves by distancing ourselves from what we think we know.

We would misjudge this process if we experience it as a duality. These two ways are in continual mutual interaction. We can deny something in the sense of internalising it in silence, only because something has been spoken. We can take the way back because there is a ladder as God first descended. It would not be possible for us to take the ascending or the descending way, if the descent, the way of revelation, had not first been there. We can view human beings as moving between both these ways. These ways grow into something like a heavenly hierarchy, but seen from the earth and having come about on earth. This, said Dionysius the Areopagite, is only possible through the mystery that Paul experienced: the indwelling of the Risen One in each of us.

The heavenly hierarchy and the church hierarchy

We can also regard the steps, the unfolding of God toward humanity, from another point of view, namely as the workings of the hierarchies of angels. It is interesting to note that in the first centuries of Christianity the angelic hierarchies were still taken for granted. One could almost say that it was common experience that many people – not only in the Christian cultures – shared. But the culmination of Dionysius' work lies in the fact that he placed the angelic hierarchy within Christianity, within the relationship between the Trinity and humanity. The angelic hierarchy is placed between the Son and the incarnation on the one hand, and on the other allows human beings a way back to the divine.

Parallel to the *Celestial Hierarchy,* Dionysius wrote the *Ecclesiastical Hierarchy* about the church hierarchy. Church hierarchy is an expression of a certain way of relating between people. Dionysius described how among people there is a kind of relationship in which someone who has been able to develop something can communicate it step by step to someone who was not yet able to do this. The receiver can then in turn develop it and pass it on to a further person. Here again we see how something that, developed by humanity, is handed on step by step.

How is the principle of development handed down from step to step? Dionysius said that those who occupy a rank that enables them to hand something down to those who stand on lower ranks, can only do this if they themselves have made corresponding steps on the ascending way – the way of emptying, detaching and distancing. The only circumstance that gives human beings the right to hand something down to another, is that they themselves seek the ascending way. Only in that case can a church hierarchy be a mirror on earth of the heavenly hierarchy.

The higher one rises in the heavenly hierarchies, the greater are the sacrifices one is asked to bring. This means that the higher beings, by their sacrifices, have been able to develop substance that can then be handed down to hierarchies below them, for what is handed down comes out of their essential being. The result is that only those who have gone the way of emptying themselves of attachments to their own individuality, the way of sacrifice, have the right to hand something down to those who have not yet progressed as far on their way.

Dionysius called this process of handing over, this reciprocity between descending and ascending ways, by the word *sacrament*. This then raises the question, what is a sacrament? Dionysius posited that a sacrament can only work if those who serve it are on the ascending way of self-emptying. If not, when they serve a sacrament, there is nothing to be shared; there is no substance that can be handed on. In the western church this has been a subject of debate and discussion for centuries. But it is important to realise that this ritual act, in which something is handed on from one being to another in ever increasing silence, is an event that can take place among human beings in any type of community.

Finally, we may ask ourselves whether the unspeakable mystery, in which shows Dionysius' connection with Paul most clearly – the mystery he always returned to and called the mystery of the unknown god who has made himself known through the Son – was an experience Dionysius himself had of the Risen Christ. In relation to this I want to quote a sentence from Dionysius' third letter. Speaking about the *Logos,* the Word, but also the Son, Dionysius wrote:

> The Word that was spoken by the Father and could incarnate in a human being remains unspeakable, and that which I have comprehended and known remains unknowable.[3]

Thus we hear a call from this impressive figure in early Christianity, a figure who was a direct follower of Paul, to continue in the direction of this mystery of Christianity, to a future which is still hiding as yet unknown treasures.

9
Origen: A Life in Service of Wisdom
Bastiaan Baan

Some of those who are in the power of the devil and follow the way of evil, will one day in the future turn to the good.

Origen, On First Principles

Peter, Paul and John

In the previous chapters we tried to trace the sources of Christianity by searching for the footprints of the great apostles Peter, Paul and John. Which pre-Christian streams prepared for their work? How did they manifest in the time of Christ? And how can we recognise their workings in early Christianity?

Perhaps it has become evident from the foregoing that each of these three streams has its necessary limitations. No single one encompasses everything. After all, Christianity is much greater than one apostle and one stream.

We have seen that Peter was particularly influenced by the embodiment of the Messiah, 'the incarnation of the Word'. In the language of the New Testament: 'And the Word became flesh' (Jn 1:14). Imagine that Christianity existed only in the realm of soul and spirit, that Jesus Christ had not been a man of flesh and blood, then something essential would be missing in Christianity. In early Christianity there was a heretical movement in which it was taught that Christ had not lived in a physical body, but only in the semblance of a body, and that his suffering was only apparent. It was called docetism (from the Greek *dokein,* to seem). The Apostles' Creed proclaims the exact opposite: 'suffered under Pontius Pilate, was crucified, died, and was buried.' Petrine Christianity describes the physical foundation of Christianity, just as the physical world is in a certain sense the foundation of our existence.

The apostle Paul, who had not known Jesus in his earthly life, described how Christ can be born in the human soul. In Paul's work, Christianity culminates in the great 'Song of Love' (1 Cor 13). He poses the decisive question: how is Christ born in the human soul?

The third of the great apostles, John, stands in the stream of spiritual Christianity. The early Christians called the Gospel of John the spiritual gospel.

Three prepositions can illustrate the particular nature of each of the three apostles.

- Christ died *for* us – Peter
- Christ is born *in* us – Paul
- Christ works *through* us – John

John's inspiration, which comes from the spirit, does not point to the origin (Peter) or the present (Paul), but points in a certain sense to the future. His writings lead to the future image of the New Jerusalem, the spiritualisation of the earth. Thus these three streams of Christianity have a relationship with body, soul and spirit, but also with the three persons of the Trinity.

- Peter is the apostle of the Father God ('You have not received this revelation from the world of the senses but from the world of my Father in the heavens,' Mt 16:17)
- Paul is the apostle of the Son God; he emphasises 'sonship' (Rom 8:23)
- John is the apostle of the Spirit God; he received the revelation of the future of creation

In the Act of Consecration of Man, this triad appears in three phrases in which, in a certain sense, all of Christianity is summarised. The text of the Act of Consecration of Man speaks of 'Christ's suffering and death, his resurrection, his revelation'. In these three words, which are spoken during the transubstantiation, the quintessence of Christianity is stated.

- His suffering and death: Peter confesses to the birth, life and death of Christ on earth
- His resurrection: Paul is the apostle of the resurrection
- His revelation: John is the apostle of the Book of Revelation (Apocalypse)

The life of Origen

The church father Origen (185–255) was an important representative of early spiritual Christianity. He was one of the greatest thinkers of early Christianity. He played a crucial role in the development of Christianity because he absorbed and reflected the best ideas of that noteworthy time. We shall look at some of the highlights of his life and his teaching. Despite his living in a far distant past, we will recognize something in it that is of importance for the further development of Christianity in our own time.

The great church historian, Eusebius (*c.* 260–338), wrote, 'The life of Origen appears to me to be interesting even from his cradle.' He undoubtedly wanted to indicate with this that he recognised the great individuality in Origen from his childhood on.

Origen was born in Alexandria in AD 185 as the eldest son of Christian parents of Greek descent. From the beginning, his life bore the stamp of Christian and Greek culture. This enabled him later to understand Christianity through Greek thinking, and to Christianise Greek thinking, These two cultural influences needed each other in a special way.

Origen's Greek name *Hōrigenēs* means *Son of Horus,* the Egyptian god with the head of a falcon. In those days it was common in Alexandria for Christians to be baptised with a pagan name. His father was a teacher, and taught his own son. From his childhood, Origen was particularly receptive to the Bible, although he did not blindly accept the stories, but would ask questions. He wanted to know the deeper significance of a story. His father would reprimand him to silence his questioning, but grew increasingly amazed and rejoiced at his son's talents.

In childhood Origen also became a pupil of Clement of Alexandria (150–*c.* 215) whom one could call his spiritual father. With remarkable clarity and in a completely natural way Origen was able to take in and absorb the substance of Christianity and pre-Christian cultures. He felt that he was of a kindred spirit with Clement. Until then, Origen seemed to be a talented, clear thinker predestined to express Christianity in philosophical terms. But then events conspired to enhance his capacities.

His father was a Christian man of action. In those days that meant that you were never sure of your life. Under successive emperors there were periods of tolerance and periods of persecution of Christians. During one of the periods of persecution Origen's father was arrested and tortured. More than anything else, Origen, who was then 15 or 16, wanted to follow his father into prison. His mother prevented this by hiding his clothes, so he was forced to stay at home. But from the moment Origen saw this example he longed for martyrdom. It seems as if he wanted to hurl himself recklessly into danger. His conviction burned in him. His fiery feelings show in a letter the young Origen wrote to his father in prison. He implored his father, 'Please mind that you don't change your persuasion for our sake. Go through fire for your faith'. A child wrote that to his father! The father followed the advice of his precocious son and died as one of the early martyrs. After his death all his possessions were confiscated. The family was split up and the children were distributed over several families.

Origen was 18 years old when he was appointed to be Clement's successor. Clement of Alexandria fled during the next persecution of Christians, for good reason. He was the leader of the Catechetical School of Alexandria, the school for Christians. Origen now had this exposed position and taught Christianity to people who were usually older than he. According to historians, it is a miracle that he did not lose his life during the persecutions under the next emperor. Not only did he occupy this lonely post, he also appeared in public. He stayed close to the Christians from his school who were persecuted and imprisoned, tortured and condemned to death. He visited them in the prisons, and just before their execution he embraced them as a sign of connectedness. For this offence he was almost stoned; he barely managed to escape – a furious mob followed him.

Clement had fled not out of fear. He later wrote to Origen that by becoming a martyr you turn your persecutors into criminals. Perhaps you can help them too by staying out of their sight. You are co-responsible for what the perpetrators do to you. A lofty, conscientious view of martyrdom! That is why Clement fled to Asia Minor. As we shall see, Origen later followed the example of his teacher.

There have probably been few Christians who lived in such complete surrender to and absolute faith in the spiritual world as Origen. His future as a brilliant scholar seemed assured. But his path became an active Christianity of deeds. He went through fire for Christianity or, literally, through icy cold. He walked barefoot through the streets of the city for years, summer and winter; he lived extremely frugally and did not spare himself. During the day he taught in his school, and devoted the nights to study. He did not sleep much.

For twenty-eight years he worked on a colossal study, unequalled in Christianity. This entailed learning Hebrew. He was on of the first 'hunters of manuscripts', searching for original specimens. He received help in this from his pupil Ambrose, a wealthy Alexandrian who made his fortune available to collect manuscripts. For twenty-eight years he collected precious manuscripts from the beginnings of Christianity and the time that preceded it. He compared the Septuagint (the Greek translation of the Old Testament) with the Hebrew and with four other translations of the Bible. This resulted in the *Hexapla* (the sixfold) in which the Hebrew, the Hebrew transliterated into Greek, and four Greek translations were placed side by side. Origen, like a thorough researcher, compared the texts with each other.

He wrote commentaries on all the important books of the Old and New Testaments. So breathtaking was the speed of his dictation that he had to employ seven speed-writers who rotated in the task. Besides the seven speed-writers, there were seven calligraphers – tradition reports that the speed-writers were men and the calligraphers women. It all took place with fiery zeal, urged by Ambrose whom Origen once compared with an Egyptian slave driver.

Later, St Jerome said, 'Origen wrote more than another person can read in his whole life'. More than a thousand homilies of his were written down; he is called the father of homilies. A homily is an explanation, a description of the background of a ritual text or Bible text. He had his scribes note them down, and it was said that he started this only after his sixtieth year, when he had perfectly mastered the art of speech. He was then, apparently without preparation, with great presence of mind and focused on a single sentence or bible text, able to dictate a perfect homily. It is said that he left six thousand works. However, his work was later considered heretical and destroyed, so that much was lost. Today only some twenty-five works from this gigantic oeuvre are extant or have been reconstructed from translations.

Origen was perhaps the greatest thinker of early Christianity. But more than a thinker, he was also a Christian of action. When the next emperor, Caracalla, started persecuting the Christians again, he was tested. Now, at a more advanced age, and perhaps also more sober-minded, Origen left Alexandria and settled in Caesarea in Palestine. There he had become so famous that – unheard of at the time – he lectured bishops. The layman was giving instruction to the highest dignitaries.

After a brief return to Alexandria in a period of calm, he was asked by the mother of the new emperor, Severus Alexander, to come to Antioch and instruct her in Christianity. This was decisive for the development of Christianity in this period. Thanks to his teaching, she was able to exert influence on her son so that during his reign Christians were left in peace. Indirectly, Origen thus contributed to unhindered spread of Christianity during the years 222 to 235.

Time and again Origen was called to travel to combat certain forms of heresy. During those journeys new possibilities opened up, but there were also complications. For instance, on a journey through Palestine on the way to Greece – he was probably around 47 years old – he was ordained as a priest by one of the bishops in Palestine, to the displeasure of his own bishop in Alexandria, Demetrius. Demetrius felt passed over, and tried in all kinds of ways to hinder Origen. When he came back to Alexandria, the 'case of Origen' was discussed in the synod and he was excommunicated. In a next synod his ordination was declared invalid, so that his priesthood was no longer recognised in Alexandria. Bishop Demetrius spread all kinds of insinuations, one of which had a particularly dubious origin.

It was said – and this does not come from Origen himself, but from contemporaries – that in excessive youthful zeal he castrated himself for the kind of reason mentioned in the Gospel of Matthew, 'there are eunuchs who have made themselves eunuchs for the sake of the kingdom of heaven' (Mt 19:12, RSV). Eusebius suspected that Origen had castrated himself. Origen himself, however, said about this Bible passage that it should not be interpreted in a physical but in a spiritual sense. I will come back later to these (physical or spiritual) interpretations. Be this as it may, all kinds of insinuations were spread about Origen. However, the decision to declare his ordination invalid was not acknowledged outside Alexandria. When he was persecuted again, he had to leave Alexandria once more and settled in Caesarea where he had stayed before. There he was finally left alone. At this stage Origen could honestly say, 'I wish the best for my persecutors and pray for them', just as Paul said, 'Bless those who persecute you' (Rom 12:14). Coming out of one of the darkest periods of his life, he recognised the good in the evil he went through.

In Caesarea he began a new life. He founded a Catechetical School which spread its fame throughout the Christian world. One of his pupils, who studied with him for five years, wrote:

> Not only was he a master in communicating and interpreting wisdom, but he was like an experienced gardener who, before he puts seed into the earth, cultivates the soil. In our Catechetical School the soil is thus ploughed, harrowed and made so receptive in the souls of the students that the precious seed of wisdom can indeed germinate and blossom.

Origen prepared this process by the study of logic. To us this sounds boring and dry, but in early Christianity logic was a most interesting, spiritual matter. In those days, dialectics, mathematics and all forms of Greek learning had the purpose of making the soul receptive to the spirit. In this study, just as in the classical mystery schools, the soul was formed and purified, it experienced catharsis. Certain virtues were practiced; the will was strengthened. In brief, in all these different ways the students worked upon themselves, beginning with clear thinking, followed by the life of habit and the will. The preparatory part of this method also included a review of the great Greek thinkers. Origen knew them and valued them. He taught philosophy in such a way that he always showed the relative truth of a particular point of view. And in the end, for him all philosophical streams led to Christianity as the crown of classical philosophy.

PART III: EARLY CHRISTIAN MOVEMENTS

Once again Origen had to live through a time of persecution of Christians. He went through an even worse trial than before, undoubtedly because of his widespread fame. In 250, under Emperor Decius, persecutions took place that required all Christians to bring a pagan sacrifice before the statue of the emperor and abjure their faith. Origen refused. He was taken prisoner and tortured. His arms and legs were stretched beyond bearing, and he was threatened with burning at the stake; but in no way could he be made to change his mind. He was finally released thanks to a benevolent judge. However, he was so injured and weakened that he had but little time left to live. Some of his students took him in and looked after him. He was no longer able to proclaim Christianity openly, but lived quietly and wrote until his death. His pupils and friends called him Adamantinos, 'made of steel, of diamond', because he had unwaveringly proclaimed Christianity.

For almost three hundred years, his teaching spread over the eastern Mediterranean world. The great teachers of the fourth century, Dionysius the Great in Alexandria, Eusebius in Caesarea, Basil the Great were all instrumental in spreading his teaching. But less than three hundred years after his death Origen was declared a heretic by Emperor Justinian (*c.* 482–565) who persecuted all who did not conform to orthodox Christianity and had closed the Academy of Plato in Athens. Origen, in his view, proclaimed a Manichaean and Arian doctrine. A similar fate befell many church fathers and early Christians. In 553 a Council confirmed it, and Pope Vigilius also branded his work as heretical and ordered a large part of his writings to be destroyed. The rest was in a certain manner misused. Later saints, such as Anthony and Jerome, literally copied his work. While they were sanctified, the author whose work they quoted was declared a heretic.

Everything about pre-existence (life before birth), everything about the eventual redemption of the creation, was rejected. Origen's view of the resurrection as a spiritual reality and not in the flesh, was branded as heresy. Origen spoke of the resurrection in the etheric body *(aetherios)*. His view that the future creation will be a non-material, spiritual one was branded as heresy.

For a long time, Origen was forgotten or ignored. It was only in the second half of the twentieth century that his work was rediscovered. There are now large international groups of people who come together in conventions to study the work of Origen.

What is early Christianity?

Emil Bock once called early Christianity the 'Christmas season' of Christianity; the time when heaven was still open. The first three hundred years after the death of Christ were the times of glory of Christianity; a period when Christ was still able to speak in the thoughts and words of the true Christians. It is said that at that time, so soon after the Mystery of Golgotha, when some of the first Christians quoted the gospels, they took on the appearance of Jesus Christ. Suddenly he was present in the word, the thought that was spoken and heard.

According to Rudolf Steiner, early Christianity ended in the year 333. Steiner pointed out this first period to the priests of the Christian Community, and said that they had the task of going back to the sources of Christianity, because in the early church fathers Christianity found expression in its purest form. After the year 333 original Christianity was already becoming muddied. Rudolf Steiner's task to the founders of the Christian Community to study the church fathers was one of the reasons for this book.

During the life of Jesus Christ, Christianity became flesh and blood. It became visible and tangible, and came into existence. In the three hundred subsequent years humanity, bit by bit, developed consciousness of what had happened. The events of Whitsun (Peter), Damascus (Paul), Patmos (John), were moments when flashes of inspiration began to awaken in Christianity. Thus Christianity developed from being to consciousness.

Why the year 333? It was the middle of the middle. Anthroposophy distinguishes seven great cultural epochs, of which the Greek-Roman one is the central one, lasting from 747 BC to AD 1413. The midpoint of this central cultural epoch fell precisely in the year 333. In the first half, the Greek period, humanity was in a certain sense still protected under the wings of the gods. Greek culture had something heavenly, certainly when compared with the second half, the Roman period, which was focused much more on the earth, where humanity had to develop consciousness of self out of its own forces.

The first half of that middle epoch was one of spiritual riches. After 333 poverty necessarily set in. The first period of Christianity was Christ's revelation. Subsequently, Christianity had to develop into thought, into dogma. It became in a certain sense incarcerated in abstract thinking. It is no coincidence that the early church fathers, such as Irenaeus, Clement and Origen, wrote their treatises in Greek, the language that was able to give expression to the spiritual. Greek was pre-eminently the language to understand Christ.

After 333 Christianity developed following the principle of individuals having to grasp it themselves. Not the revelation, but our own thinking became decisive.

Thinking about the Bible

Origen was the pre-eminent church father who, with his lucid, spiritual thinking, was able to understand what the Bible had to say. That was extremely useful, for at that time not only was the fruit of early Christianity growing, there were also all kinds of false doctrines developing, in part by misinterpretations and interpolations. Origen developed original thoughts, which were rooted in the spirituality of primal Christianity. With these thoughts – such as about the threefold significance of Scripture – he provided his readers with a key to find access to the contents of Christianity on their own. Origen recognised that the Bible only becomes truly accessible when we acknowledge and have insight in its threefold significance.

> The individual ought, then, to portray the ideas of holy Scripture in a threefold manner upon his own soul; in order that the simple man may be edified by the 'flesh,' as it were, of the Scripture, for so we name the obvious sense; while he who has ascended a certain way (may be edified) by the 'soul,' as it were. The perfect man, again, and he who resembles those spoken of by the apostle, when he says, 'We speak wisdom among them that are perfect, but not the wisdom of the world ... but we speak the wisdom of God ...' may receive edification from the spiritual law, which has a shadow of good things to come. For as man consists of body, and soul, and spirit, so in the same way does Scripture.[1]

What we distinguished in the preceding chapters as the three streams in Christianity, the Petrine, Pauline and Johannine streams, can also be recognised in the Bible. A part of the Bible expresses physical reality, another part speaks to the soul, and there is a part that should be spiritually interpreted. However, each individual part can also be read in three ways. For instance, the meeting of Mary and Elisabeth can without doubt be viewed as a concrete encounter. But the Gospel indicates that there was also a soul element, namely the joy of the meeting, which was so profound that Elisabeth's child leapt in her womb. Can we meet each other in such a way that we call forth the best in the other, so that the 'child' leaps for joy? Finally, this encounter had a spiritual significance, for because of the conversation that developed between the two women, truth and depth grew in them. This does not happen in a monologue, but by something that moves back and forth between human beings.

Be careful, said Origen, with passages in the Bible where a physical impossibility is described as if it actually happened. There Holy Scripture indicates a different meaning than physical reality. Thus something does not match physical reality when Christ said, 'If someone strikes you on the right cheek, turn the left cheek to him also' (Mt 5:39). Because in his days people were forced to be right-handed in their work and writing Origen was saying: When you are slapped, it is obviously on the left cheek. It is one of those passages with a paradox, something that does not happen in the physical world – therefore it has another meaning. When someone does something to you on your active (right) side, turn your receptive (left) side to him also. In this way there are many passages that in the course of time have become incomprehensible but, when considered in the light of the threefold significance of Scripture, can be made accessible anew.

Why is this so important? In the history of theology Christianity has in our own time become more and more reduced. This development has sometimes mockingly been called the one-page Bible. One page suffices for everything in the Bible that can be historically verified. Christianity is reduced to the story of the simple carpenter Jesus of Nazareth. Everything else that is so paradoxical and enigmatic is eliminated, until in the twentieth century a form of fundamentalism develops that took everything literally, purely materialistically. Every word, every sentence is interpreted in a materialistic sense. In the views of Christian fundamentalism the Book of Revelation becomes a violent battlefield against the 'axis of evil'. In some sects, the New Jerusalem is represented as a land of milk and honey with dining tables beautifully set and first class service. In such interpretations the intention of John the Evangelist is in fact thwarted and contradicted.

Rudolf Steiner apparently foresaw this development and said that in the course of the twentieth century a form of Christianity would develop in some circles that interprets everything in the Bible in a physical way.

> People who have lost all trace of true Christianity will call themselves Christians, and they will rage against those who do not exclusively adhere to what Christ said according to the tradition of the gospels, but who hold to the words, 'I am in your midst all the days until the completion of earthly time' (Mt 28:20), and who are guided by the living, always active Christ impulse.[2]

The danger of new forms of Christian fundamentalism is that soul and spirit no longer play a role – and that the Bible is interpreted literally. This method, said Steiner, serves the opposite purpose of Christianity.

Origin and future

Johannine Christianity looks in a certain sense to the origin with its eye on the future, because it is orientated principally on the future ('I am the first and the last,' Rev. 1:17). In Origen, the principle of freedom of will is present from the beginning of creation. God is the eternal Creator. New creations continually come into being through him. The beginning of Creation took place in the realm of invisibility. God first created what Genesis calls the 'sons of God'. These sons of God – we call them the angelic hierarchies – developed further following the principle of free will, or they remained behind in their development. The hierarchies also went through a stage of free choice that can be compared with that of the human being. Some of them remained behind in their development, following the principle of 'to rest is to rust'. Actually, that is the origin of evil: I am not going with you; I am staying where I am! In this way, some of the hierarchies separated off and rebelled. Origen wrote:

> Because these creatures, who are endowed with reason [the sons of God], possess free will, each of them is free either to develop to the good in the footsteps of God, or in opposition to turn away from him. This is the reason for the inequality among spiritual beings.[3]

The human being is pulled along in this development, at least in part. Origen said that we can recognise the fall into sin in the Greek word that is used to indicate the human soul. Now we enter into a peculiar etymology in the Greek language. The word *psychē* (soul) is related to *psychos* (cold, frost). The verb *psychein* in its active form means to blow, to breathe. God 'breathed' the soul into Adam. Breath and *psychē* are the same. But in its passive form, this verb means to cool off. The fall into sin consists of a cooling off. The fire that flamed up in the human being because of God's breath disappears under ashes; it is covered over. The soul cools off, figuratively speaking. But, said Origen, the human soul has the potential to return to its original condition. It is not completely extinguished; by working on itself the soul can become warm again. This spiritual glow is clearly recognisable in Origen.

The same process takes place on a macrocosmic level in creation. Origen used a particular term when the creation is mentioned in the Old and New Testaments: *katabolē kosmou* – literally the ordered creation that has sunk into the depths. According to Origen, all creation came into being out of warmth and subsequently condensed into light, air, liquid and rigid earth. From these separate states the way back begins; a way that is in a certain sense a way forward, not back to paradise, but to what Origen called the restoration of all things. He used a term for this that was declared heretical by established Christianity, but that appears in the New Testament. In Acts 3:21, Peter wrote of the restoration of all things *(apokatastasis pantōn)*. In the context of this speech, Peter did not mean a going back to what was in the past but a new wholeness, which has to be prepared by an about-face, a thorough change of attitude (Acts 3:19).

Christ laid in the human being, like a hidden seed, the potential of becoming 'God', becoming a future hierarchy: 'You are gods' (Jn 10:34). *Apokatastasis pantōn* – this is the spiritualisation of the creation that must take place not only in ourselves; while every person has to work on it, sooner or later the entire creation participates in it. According to Origen this restoration will occur even for 'some [of the spirits] who are under the dominion of the devil and follow the way of evil'. A part of the creation can be restored in the sense of uncovering the germ that was once laid in us and that helps to spiritualise the creation.

Notes

Foreword
1 Schelling, *Philosophie der Offenbarung,* lectures 36 and 37.

1 The Messianic Expectation in the Old Testament
1 This history is beautifully described by Chaim Potok in *Wanderings: The History of the Jews.*
2 Finkelstein & Silberman, *The Bible Unearthed.*
3 Potok, *Wanderings: The History of the Jews.*
4 See also Steiner, *According to Matthew,* lecture of Sep 6, 1910, and *The Fifth Gospel,* lecture of Oct 3, 1913.
5 Paraphrased from Patai, *The Messiah Texts.*
6 The Hebrew Book of Enoch (Enoch 3), 45:5.
7 The Zohar, quoted from Bock, *The Childhood of Jesus,* p. 86.
8 Bock, *The Childhood of Jesus,* pp. 34ff.
9 Note that the destinies of the two Jesus children are the reverse of those of the Messianic expectations, where it is the Messiah-ben-Joseph who died and was brought to life again by the Messiah-ben-David.
10 Weinreb, *Das Buch Jona.*

2 Mysteries and Initiation in the Greek World
1 *Phaedo* 13 (tr. Sanderson Beck).
2 Plutarch, *On the Decline of the Oracles.*

3 Messianic Expectation and the Essenes
1 Steiner, *The Fifth Gospel,* lecture of Dec 17, 1913, pp. 198f.
2 Philo, *On the Contemplative Life,* X.76f.
3 Philo, *On the Contemplative Life,* XI.88f.
4 Philo, *On the Contemplative Life,* IV.35.
5 Steiner, *According to Matthew,* lecture of Sep 5, 1910, p. 82.
6 Steiner, *According to Matthew,* lecture of Sep 6, 1910, p. 102.
7 'The Community Rule,' Vermes, *The Dead Sea Scrolls in English,* p. 72.
8 Steiner, *According to Matthew,* lecture of Sep 10, 1910, p.178.

4 Peter, the Builder of Churches

1. *Acts of Peter,* 35, from James, *Apocryphal New Testament,* p. 333.
2. See Steiner, *According to Matthew,* lecture of Sep 11, 1910.
3. *Gospel of Peter,* V.19, from James, *Apocryphal New Testament,* p. 91.
4. Irenaeus, *Against Heresies,* I.26.2.
5. Ohlig, K.-H., 'Das Syrische und Arabische Christentum und der Koran' in Ohlig & Puin, *Die dunklen Anfänge.*
6. Walsh, M., *The Roots of Christianity.*
7. Quispel, *Tatian and the Gospel of Thomas.*
8. *Letter of Christ and Abgarus,* from James, *Apocryphal New Testament,* p. 477.
9. *Acts of Thomas,* I.11, from James, *Apocryphal New Testament,* p. 369.
10. This and following quotes from *Gospel of Thomas,* tr. T. Lambdin from www.earlychristianwritings.com
11. Schaik, *Why Jesus Didn't Marry Mary Magdalene.*
12. Douglas-Klotz, *The Hidden Gospel.*
13. Birnie, *The Synod of Mar Dadiso* (44, 50), also Chabot, *Synodicon Orientale ou Recueil de Synodes Nestoriens,* pp. 285f.

6 John: The Imitation of Christ

1. Thomas Aquinas, *Commentary on the Gospel of St John,* Ch. 21, 2638.
2. Jerome, in his *Commentaries on Galatians.*
3. Steiner, *The Gospel of St John,* lecture of May 22, 1908, p. 64.
4. Origen, *Commentary on the Gospel of St John.*
5. Johann Valentin Andreae, 'Fama Fraternitatis' in Allen, *A Christian Rosenkreutz Anthology.*
6. Origen, *Commentary on the Gospel of St John.*
7. Steiner, *Kosmogonie,* lecture of Oct 28, 1906, p. 245.
8. Bamford, *The Voice of the Eagle,* p. 76.
9. Thomas Aquinas, *Commentary on the Gospel of St John,* Ch. 11, 1533.

7 Esoteric Petrine Christianity

1. See Steiner, *Broken Vessels,* lecture of Sep 18, 1924, and *The Spiritual Ground of Education,* lecture of August 18, 1922.
2. Rudolf Steiner, *According to Matthew,* lecture of 11 Sep1910, p. 189.
3. This and the following quotations from 'Life Simeon the Stylite,' in Theodoret, *Religious History.*
4. This agrees with Rudolf Steiner's words: prerequisite for this path is that one has a strong etheric body so that the physical body can recuperate relatively quickly (see *Broken Vessels*).
5. Athanasius, *Life of Antony.*
6. 'Elisabeth von Schönau' in Dinzelbacher, *Vision und Visionsliteratur im Mittelalter.*

7   This and subsequent Celano quotations, from Thomas of Celano, *The Life of St Francis of Assisi.*

8 Dionysius the Areopagite, the First Christian Mystic

1   Paraphrased. For modern translation see Luibheid, *Pseudo-Dionysius: The Complete Works.*
2   Stein, *Wege der Gotteserkenntnis.*
3   Paraphrased. For modern translation see Luibheid, *Pseudo-Dionysius: The Complete Works.*

9 Origen: A Life in Service of Wisdom

1   Origen, *On First Principles,* Book IV, 11.
2   Rudolf Steiner, March 7, 1914, p. 4. Notes from an unpublished lecture, *www.uranosarchiv.de.*
3   Origen, *On First Principles,* Book IV.

Bibliography

Allen, Paul M., *A Christian Rosenkreutz Anthology,* Rudolf Steiner Publications 1968.
Aquinas, *see* Thomas Aquinas
Baan, Bastiaan, *Old and New Mysteries,* Floris Books 2014.
Bamford, Christopher, *The Voice of the Eagle: Homily on the Prologue to the Gospel of St John by John Scotus Eriugena,* Lindisfarne Press 1990.
Barnstone, Willis (ed.), *The Other Bible,* Harper San Francisco 2005.
Becking, B. & Dijkstra, M. (eds.), *Een God alleen? Over monotheisme in Oud-Israel en de verering van de godin Asjera,* Kampen 1998.
Birnie, M.J., *The Synod of Mar Dadiso* AD *424* (unpublished) www.fourthcentury.com/the-council-of-mar-dadiso-ad-424/
Bock, Emil, *Caesars and Apostles: Hellenism, Rome and Judaism,* Floris Books 1997.
—, *The Childhood of Jesus,* Floris Books 1997.
—, *Saint Paul: Life, Epistles and Teachings,* Floris Books 1993.
—, *Studies in the Gospels* (2 vols.) Floris Books 2009, 2011.
—, *The Three Years: The Life of Christ between Baprism and Ascension,* Floris Books 1980.
Brock, Sebastian, *Studies in Syriac Christianity,* Variorum, UK 1992.
Celano, *see* Thomas of Celano
Chabot, J.B. (ed. & tr.), *Synodicon Orientale ou Recueil de Synodes Nestoriens,* Paris 1902.
Dinzelbacher, Peter, *Vision und Visionsliteratur im Mittelalter,* Stuttgart 1981.
Douglas-Klotz, Neil, *The Hidden Gospel. Decoding the Spiritual Message of the Aramaic Jesus,* Quest, USA 1999.
Dunn James, D.G., *The Cambridge Companion to St Paul,* Cambridge University Press 2003.
Finkelstein, I. & Silberman, N. A., *The Bible Unearthed: Archeology's New Vision of Ancient Israel and the Origin of its Sacred Texts,* New York 2001.
Frieling, Rudolf, *New Testament Studies,* Floris Books 1994.
Halle, J. von, *And if He has Not Been Raised: the Stations of Christ's Path to Spirit Man,* Temple Lodge, UK 2007.
Hebrew Book of Enoch (Enoch 3) archive.org/stream/HebrewBookOfEnochenoch3/BookOfEnoch3_djvu.txt

Hemleben, Johannes, *Der Evangelist Johannes,* Rowohlt 1972.
Hiebel, F., *The Gospel of Hellas,* Anthroposophic Press, USA 1949.
James, Montague Rhodes (tr.) *The Apocryphal New Testament,* Oxford 1924.
Kerényi, Carl, *Eleusis: Archetypal Image of Mother and Daughter,* Princeton University Press 1967.
Klockenbring, Gérard, *L'Evangile selon Jean,* Editions Iona, 1985.
Kurras, Eberhard, *Christus-Erfahrungen: Petrus, Paulus, Johannes,* Urachhaus 1975.
Luibheid, C., *Pseudo-Dionysius. The Complete Works,* Paulist Press, USA 1987.
Madsen, Jon (tr.) *The New Testament,* Floris Books 2017.
Meyer, M.W., *The Ancient Mysteries: A Sourcebook of Sacred Texts of the Mystery Religions of the Ancient Mediterranean World,* Harper San Francisco 1987.
Mitchell, M.M., *The Heavenly Trumpet: John Chrysostom and the Art of Pauline Interpretation,* Westminster Press 2002
Ohlig, K.-H. & Puin, G.-R. (eds.), *Die dunklen Anfänge: Neue Forschungen zur Entstehung und frühen Geschichte des Islam,* Hans Schiller 2005.
Origen, *Commentary on the Gospel of St John,* From *Ante-Nicene Fathers,* Vol. 4. www.newadvent.org/fathers
—, *On First Principles,* tr. Frederick Crombie. From *Ante-Nicene Fathers,* Vol. 4. www.newadvent.org/fathers/0412.htm
Patai, R., *The Messiah Texts,* Detroit 1988.
Philo, *On the Contemplative Life,* www.earlychristianwritings.com/yonge/book34.html
Plato, *Phaedo,* (tr. Sanderson Beck) www.san.beck.org/Phaedo.html
Plutarch, *On the 'E' at Delphi,* penelope.uchicago.edu/misctracts/plutarche.html.
Potok, Chaim, *Wanderings: The History of the Jews.*
Quispel, Gilles, *Tatian and the Gospel of Thomas: Studies in the History of the Western Diatesseron,* Brill, Leiden 1975.
Riemeck, Renate, *Glaube, Dogma, Macht: Geschichte der Konzilien,* Urachhaus 1985.
Schaik, J. van, *Why Jesus Didn't Marry Mary Magdalene,* Floris Books 2007.
Schelling, F.W.J. von, *Philosophie der Offenbarung,* 1854.
Stein, E. *Wege der Gotteserkenntnis: Dionysios der Areopagit und seine symbolische Theologie,* Regensburg 1979.
Steiner, Rudolf. Volume Nos refer to the Collected Works (CW), or to the German Gesamtausgabe (GA).
—, *According to Matthew* (CW 123) SteinerBooks, USA 2002.
—, *Broken Vessels: the Spiritual Structure of Human Frailty* (CW 318) SteinerBooks 2002.
—, *Christianity as Mystical Fact and the Mysteries of Antiquity* (CW 8) Anthroposophic Press, USA 1997.
—, *The Fifth Gospel: From the Akashic Record* (CW 148) Rudolf Steiner Press 1995.
—, *The Gospel of St John* (CW 103) Anthroposophic Press 1984.

—, *Kosmogonie* (GA 94), Dornach 1979.
—, *The Reappearance of Christ in the Etheric* (CW 118) SteinerBooks, USA 2004.
—, *The Spiritual Ground of Education* (CW 305) SteinerBooks, USA 2004.
Stiglmayer S.J., 'Der Neuplatoniker Proklus als Vorlage des sog. Dionysius Areopagita in der Lehre vom Übel in *Historisches Jahrbuch der Gorres-Gesellschaft,* 1895.
Theodoret of Cyrrhus, *Religious History* in *Nicene and Post-Nicene Fathers,* series II.
Thomas Aquinas, *Commentary on the Gospel of St John,* Kindle edition.
Thomas of Celano, *The Life of St Francis of Assisi and the Treatise of the Miracles* (tr. Catherine Bolton) Minerva, Assisi 2004.
Vermes, G. (ed.) *The Dead Sea Scrolls in English,* Penguin Books 1962.
Voragine, Jacobus de, *The Golden Legend* (tr. W.G. Ryan) Princeton University Press 1993.
Walsh, Michael J., *The Roots of Christianity,* Grafton 1986.
Weinreb, Friedrich, *Das Buch Jona,* Bern 1986.
Welburn, Andrew, *The Beginnings of Christianity,* Floris Books 2007.
Welburn, A., *The Mysteries: Rudolf Steiner's Writings on Spiritual Initiation,* Floris Books 1996.
Wright, D., *The Eleusinian Mysteries and Rites,* London 1919 (reprinted Kessinger 2010).

Glossary and Index

Abel 109
Abgar V, King 68
Abgar IX, King 65
Addai (Thaddeus of Edessa) 68
adoptionism 65, 71
agapē 99–102, 106
Alexander the Great (356–327 BC, King of Macedonia, united Greek city-states, conquered Persia and Egypt) 15, 29
Alexandria 145, 148
Alexius of Rome, St (fifth century) 121
Allah 72
Ambrose of Alexandria (d. 250) 147
Anthony, St 120, 150
Antioch 60, 63f, 148
Apollo (Greek god of beauty and order, son of Zeus and Leto) 33
Apollonius of Tyana 81
apophatic way 140
Areopagus in Athens 93, 127
Aristotle (384–322 BC, Greek philosopher, teacher of Alexander the Great, founder of formal logic and the doctrine of categories of being) 28, 33, 36
Aristophanes (*c.* 445–*c.* 388 BC, Greek playwright) 36
Arius (256–336, Christian teacher of Arianism) 73
Askesis (preparation of athletes for the Olympic Games which also contained religious elements)
Astarte (Asherah) 13f
Athanasius (*c.* 296–373, bishop of Alexandria) 73

Athens 92, 94f, 127, 129
Augustine of Hippo (Aurelius Augustinus, 354–430, Christian theologian, influential on western thinking) 131

Baal 13
Baan, Bastiaan 88, 91
Barnabas (early Christian, companion of St Paul) 61
Basil the Great (330–379, Greek bishop of Caesarea Mazaca) 150
Bock, Emil 80f, 83, 87, 151
Boethius (480–525, Roman philosopher and politician, translator of Plato and Aristotle in Latin) 131

Caesarea in Palestine 148f
Caesarea Philippi 62
Cain 109
Cana, marriage at 67, 108
Caracalla (188–217, Roman emperor, son of Septimius Severus; notorious for his atrocities and extravagance) 148
Catechetical School of Alexandria 146, 149
Celeus, King 35
Chalcedonian Creed 74
Charles the Bald, King 133
Christianity
—, orthodox 131
—, Roman 131
Christology 88
Church of the East 74f
circumcision 60

Clement of Alexandria
    (c. 150–c. 215, church father,
    head of the Catechetical School of
    Alexandria) 40f, 65, 132, 145–47
Clement (c. 35–99, Bishop of Rome) 61
Cloud of Unknowing 132
Constantinople 131

Damaris (priestess of Eleusis) 94, 128
Damascus 85
Damian, Peter (c. 1007–72, reforming
    Benedictine monk) 121
David, King 17f, 20
Dead Sea Scrolls 46
Decius, Emperor 150
Delphi (the most famous mystery centre
    in ancient Greece) 33, 38
Demeter (sister of Zeus, goddess of
    agriculture and fertility) 33–35, 38
Demetrius of Alexandria (d. c. 230) 148
Denis, St (third-century martyr, first
    bishop of Paris) 132f
Dionysius the Areopagite 36, 39, 94f,
    128–33, 136–38, 140–42
Dionysius, Pseudo- 95, 134
Dionysius the Great in Alexandria 150
Dionysus (Greek god of viticulture and
    fertility, dance and life; son of Zeus
    and Semele)
docetism 143
Domitian, Emperor 111f

Ebionites 65f
Edessa (now Urfa, Turkey) 65–68, 121
Elcesaites (sect) 66
Elchasai (Jewish 'prophet') 66
Eleusis (Greek mystery centre dedicated
    to Demeter and Persephone) 33–36,
    38
Elijah 13, 24
Elisabeth of Schönau 122
Elisabeth (mother of John the Baptist)
    153
Elohists 15
Emmerich, Anne Catherine (1774–
    1824, German Augustinian nun who
    received the stigmata and had visions
    of Christ) 110
Encratites 67, 115–7, 119
Ephesus 110–12
Epicureans (Greek philosophy searching
    for relationship between free will,
    lust and suffering, founded by
    Epicurus 342–270 BC) 127
Epiphanius of Salamis (c. 315–403) 65
Eriugena, John Scotus
    (c. 810–877, theologian at the court
    of Charles the Bald) 105, 133
Essenes 45–51, 53–55
Eusebius (c. 260–340, Greek historian
    of Christianity) 63, 65, 145, 149f

Francis of Assisi, St 122, 124–6
Friend of God from the Oberland
    (figure from fourteenth-century
    mystical stream to which Johannes
    Tauler and Heinrich Suso belonged)
    132

Gallio, Proconsul 79
Gamaliel (d. AD 52, leading authority in
    the Sanhedrin, teacher of St Paul) 82f
Gaon, Rabbi 19
Gnostics (wide range of religious and
    mystical streams concerned with the
    lost connection of humans to the
    divine) 42, 66
— movements 30
Golden Legend, The 100
Greek language 28f, 41f, 77, 131

Halle, Judith von 125
Hasmonean 21
Heracles (or Hercules, son of Zeus
    and Alcmene, famous for his twelve
    labours)
Heraclitus (c. 540 BC Greek pre-Socratic
    philosopher) 28
Hexapla (Hebrew & Greek Old
    Testament) 147
hierarchies, heavenly 141
hierarchy, Church 141

GLOSSARY AND INDEX

hierophant (priest in mystery temple who performs the mystery acts) 37
Hildegard of Bingen 122, 126
Hillel the Elder (*c.* 110 BC – AD 10, Jewish scholar, head of the Sanhedrin, founder of a famous liberal rabbinical school) 82
Hippolytus of Rome (170–235, theologian and the first counter-pope, adversary of Gnostics, prosecuted and venerated as a martyr) 40
homoousion 73

Iacchus (mystery name of Dionysus) 36, 38f
Ignatius of Antioch (bishop 70–107) 63
image and archetype 90
India 68f
initiation 32f, 38, 41, 88
Irenaeus 61, 65
Irenaeus of Lyon 115
Isaiah scroll 53
Islam 75
Israel (Jacob) 24

Jacob (son of Isaac) 24
James, the brother of the Lord (the Righteous) 65, 70
James the Lesser 60, 63
Jerome, St (*c.* 340–420, church father, translated Bible into Latin, the Vulgate) 64f, 147, 150
Jesus of Nazareth 86f, 101
—, genealogies of 23
John the Evangelist 74, 82f, 97, 99, 100–102, 104–109, 111f, 144
John of Damascus, St (676–749, monk, theologian) 132
John-Hyrcanus I 21
John Scotus Eriugena, *see* Eriugena, John Scotus
Joseph, son of Jacob 20, 24
Josephus Flavius (AD 37–*c.* 100, Jewish historian) 50
Joshua, priest 18f
Judas Thomas 69

Julian the Apostate (331–363, Roman Emperor, born a Christian but tried to restore pre-Christian worship and tradition) 42
Justinian (Emperor of Byzantium 527–565) 29, 150

kataphatic way 140
Kerala, church in 69
Koch, Hugo 133f

Latin 41, 131
Lazarus 100, 105f, 110
Leo IX, Pope 121
Logos 29, 33, 40–43, 73, 80, 132, 134, 142

Malachi 15, 24
Mandaeans 66
Mani 66
Mar Dadiso 72f
Martha 111
Mary (mother of Jesus) 101f, 110f, 153
Maximus the Confessor (580–662, church father, persecuted for his Christological views, later venerated in east and west) 130, 132
Melchizedek 21, 107
Messiah 16, 20
—, kingly 16f, 22, 54
—, priestly 16f, 22, 54
Messiah-ben-David 20, 23f
Messiah-ben-Joseph 20, 22–24
Michael II (770–829, Byzantine Emperor) 133
Monarchianism 73
Monophysite 72, 74, 130
monotheism 14f
Moses 14
mysteries 43
—, greater 37–40
—, lesser 35–37

Nazarenes 65f
Nazareth 110
Nazir 50

Nazirite (one who dedicated himself to the Lord, vowing to refrain from intoxicating drink, cutting hair, etc.) 49f
Neapolis (now Kavala in NE Greece on Aegean Sea) 129
Nestorian Church 64, 72f
Nestorius (c. 386–c. 450, Archbishop of Constantinople) 73f
Neumann, Therese 125

Odysseus (hero of Homer's *Odyssey* about his wanderings after the Trojan War) 32
Olympus, Mount 129
Origen (185–254, church father, defender of Christianity in the third century, sought synthesis between Old Testament revelation and Greek thinking) 65, 102, 104, 132, 145–56

Pan (Greek God) 30, 39
Patmos 112
Paul, St 42, 60–62, 65, 74, 77–95, 97, 127–29, 130, 134–37, 139f 142, 144
Pearl, Hymn of the 71
Persephone 34f, 38
Peter, St 23, 59, 60–63, 73, 83, 89, 97, 117, 143f, 155
—, Acts of 68
Peter Damian 121
Philo of Alexandria (c. 20 BC–AD 50, Jewish-Hellenistic philosopher) 46–48, 77
Philosophers' Stone 110
Plato (c. 427–c. 347 BC, Greek philosopher who considered knowledge of ideas as the only true knowledge) 28, 33, 40
Plato, Academy of (Athenian school founded by Plato in 387 BC) 29
Pliny the Elder 48
Plutarch (c. 46–c. 120, Greek biographer, priest of Apollo in Delphi) 33, 38
Proclus (411–485, Neoplatonic philosopher and mathematician) 133
Pseudo-Dionysius 95, 134

Pythagoras (c. 569–c. 507 BC, Greek philosopher) 28
Pythia (oracle priestess in the sanctuary of Apollo in Delphi, Greece)

Qumran 48f, 52–54

Raphael (artist) 93, 99
Rome 61f
—, church of 64, 74
Rosenkreutz, Christian 104

Sabians 66
sacrament 142
Saintes-Maries-de-la-Mer, France 111
Sanhedrin 82
Scotus Eriugena, *see* Eriugena, John Scotus
Second Coming 55f
Seneca the Younger, Lucius A. (c. 4 BC – AD 65, Roman philosopher, statesman and dramatist) 80
Septuagint (Greek translation of the Old Testament) 81
Serapion of Antioch (d. 211, patriarch of Antioch) 63
Severus of Antioch (465–538, patriarch of Antioch, exiled to Egypt due for Monophysite teaching, venerated in Syrian Church) 130
Severus Alexander, Emperor 148
Shaddai, El 14
sibyls (temple servants who foretold the future in a kind of ecstasy) 30
Simeon the Stylite 117, 119f
Simon the Magician (Simon the Sorcerer) 61
Sirens (Greek demi-goddesses with body of a bird and head of a woman, seduced travellers with song) 32
Sistine Madonna 99
Socrates (470–399 BC, eldest of the three great Greek philosophers, whose philosophy include self-knowledge, moral integrity and Socratic dialogue; condemned to death for criticism of Athenian elite) 29, 33

Son of Man 16f, 24, 54, 62
Stein, Edith (1891–1942, German Carmelite nun, later sanctified) 134
Steiner, Rudolf (1861–1925, Austrian philosopher and founder of anthroposophy) 23, 49, 50–52, 54–56, 83, 87, 102, 105, 116f, 151, 154
Stephen, St (first martyr) 77, 84
Stiglmayr, Josef 133f
Stoicism, Stoics (philosophical movement focused on virtue and reason) 31, 80, 127
Suger, Abbot (1081–1151, French cleric, architect, politician and historian, advisor to Louis VI) 133
Syriac Orthodox church 64, 66, 69, 74f

Talmud (interpretation of the *Mishna*, a third-century collection of Jewish religious laws) 19
Tarsus 80
Tatian (*c.* 120–180, Syrian theologian) 66f, 115
Temple Scroll 53
Teresa of Avila (1515–1582) 125
Tertullian (*c.* 160 – *c.* 230, church father, prolific author) 131

Theodoret (393–*c.* 460, bishop of Cyrrhus) 117
Therapeutae 46
Thessalonica 129
Thomas, St 65, 68f
—, Acts of 68, 71
—, Gospel of 67, 70
Thomas Aquinas 100, 106
Thomas de Celano 125
Timothy, St (companion of Paul) 137
transcendence 138
Trinity 73
Troy 128

unknown god 30, 93, 128, 137, 142
Urfa *see* Edessa

Vigilius, Pope 150
Voragine's 100
Yahwist 15
Yeshu-ben-Pandira 50

Zechariah (Hebrew prophet) 18–20
Zerubbabel (Persian govenor) 18f
Zohar (mystical Jewish writings) 20

For news on all our **latest books**, and to receive **exclusive discounts**, **join** our mailing list at:

florisbooks.co.uk

Plus subscribers get a FREE book with every online order!

We will never pass your details to anyone else.

Old and New Mysteries
From Trials to Initiation

Bastiaan Baan

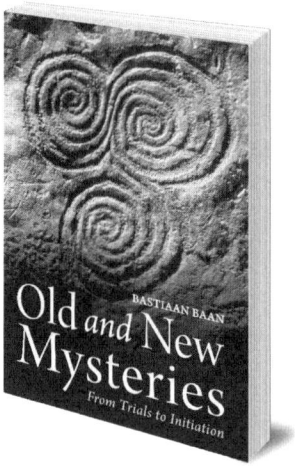

"Rich in illustrations, rich in knowledge and practical advice."
– New View

There is great contemporary interest in the mystery centres of antiquity, such as prehistoric caves, the pyramids of Egypt, Newgrange in Ireland, and the Externsteine in Germany. The trials and rites that took place there were for the chosen few, and are vividly described in this book – from the trials of fire and water to the three-day near-death sleep.

Christian Community priest Bastiaan Baan argues that modern-day initiation, however, has a substantially different character. Whereas a 'hierophant' – a guide – was previously needed to navigate a trial, these days it is life itself which brings us trials, which can sometimes lead to deeper experiences of the spiritual. between Christianity and the natural world.

florisbooks.co.uk